SEXING THE CHURCH

ALINE H. KALBIAN

SEXING THE CHURCH

GENDER, POWER, AND ETHICS IN CONTEMPORARY CATHOLICISM

INDIANA
UNIVERSITY
PRESS
Bloomington & Indianapolis

This book is a publication of

Indiana University Press
601 North Morton Street
Bloomington, IN 47404-3797 USA

http://iupress.indiana.edu

Telephone orders   800-842-6796
Fax orders   812-855-7931
Orders by e-mail   iuporder@indiana.edu

Manufactured in the United States of America

Library of Congress Cataloging-in-Publication Data

Kalbian, Aline H., date–
     Sexing the church : gender, power, and ethics in contemporary
     Catholicism / Aline H. Kalbian.
          p.   cm.
     Includes bibliographical references (p.   ) and index.
     ISBN 0-253-21750-4 (pbk. : alk. paper) — ISBN 0-253-34530-8 (cloth : alk.
paper)
     1. Sex—Religious aspects—Catholic Church.   I. Title.
BX1795.S48K36 2005
241'.66'088282—dc22   2004015475

1   2   3   4   5   10   09   08   07   06   05

With gratitude
To my parents

Ada Haddad Kalbian and Vicken Vahan Kalbian

ACKNOWLEDGMENTS *ix*

1 ORDER AND SEXUAL ETHICS *1*
2 THEOLOGY AND MARRIAGE *21*
3 REPRODUCTION *55*

CONTENTS

4 GENDER *94*
5 CONCLUSION *134*

NOTES *143*
BIBLIOGRAPHY *157*
INDEX *163*

It was my good fortune as I was writing this book to have the unwavering support of friends, family, and colleagues. In fact, I still have to pinch myself sometimes at this abundance. I am grateful to them all.

John Kelsay, my colleague, friend, and chairman in the Department of Religion at Florida State University has been my greatest champion over the past five years. In addition to allowing me the time and space to pursue my work, he has also read most of this manuscript and given me helpful input and advice at every step of the process.

Margaret Morhmann, George Randels, and James Turner Johnson all read and commented on early drafts of this manuscript. I appreciate the time and effort they took to do so.

ACKNOWLEDGMENTS

All of my colleagues in the Department of Religion, especially Shannon Burkes, John Corrigan, Bryan Cuevas, Kathleen Erndl, David Kangas, Martin Kavka, Amy Koehlinger, David Levenson, Amanda Porterfield, Leo Sandon, and Barney Twiss, have helped me in countless ways—walking to get coffee, advising me on the ins and outs of the publishing world, or just helping me keep things in perspective with their good humor. I will be forever grateful for the wonderful intellectual environment they provide. I also want to acknowledge my graduate students, whose insights and comments helped me shape many of the ideas in this book.

Many friends supported me through the writing of this book. I want to mention especially Jeff Tatum, Cathy Levenson, Jim and Ellen Shelton, Lois Shepherd, Sheila Curran, Inese Radzins, Richard Brown, and Tracy Fessenden.

As I worked on this project, two of my teachers from graduate school, Jim Childress and David Little, were never far from my mind. From both of them I learned about integrity and scholarly rigor. I am always thankful for all they taught me. They both continue to inspire me.

I have also benefited throughout from the continual love and support of my extended family, especially my sister Maral and my brother Haig.

I want to thank Bob Sloan and the staff at Indiana University Press for their careful attention to this project, and also Kate Babbitt for her copyediting and indexing skills.

Bob Cross, the center of my life for the past seventeen years, is the main reason that I was able to finish this book. He filled my life with love and humor; serenaded me with his guitar and mandolin; surrounded me with a garden filled with beautiful flowers, birds, and butterflies; and never stopped believing in me. My gratitude to him cannot be measured.

Finally, I want to dedicate this book to my parents, Ada and Vicken Kalbian; I admire them more than they can imagine. They are remarkable people who left a war-torn Palestine to give their children a safer life. They taught me a valuable lesson; that "homeland" is the world you create when you surround yourself with what matters—books, ideas, and good friends.

SEXING THE CHURCH

ORDER AND SEXUAL ETHICS 1

Sex is a contentious topic in Catholicism. Mark Jordan notes that in the contemporary American imagination, Christianity is often thought to be nothing more than a "code of sexual conduct" (Jordan 2002, 5). In other words, most Americans know little about the details of doctrines such as the trinity, the resurrection, or the incarnation, but they can recite lists of prohibitions against particular sexual acts. Jordan is clearly exaggerating for effect, yet he draws attention to an important point—that the regulation of human sexuality is central to most perceptions of Christianity.[1] In the case of Roman Catholic Christianity, the association of religion and sexuality is even more pronounced—a perception reinforced by recent attention to sexual misconduct by Catholic clergy.

The link between Christianity and sex is not limited to the public imagination. Indeed, an internal discussion among Catholic theologians is also suggestive of the central connection between modes and sources of moral reasoning in religious ethics and the regulation of human sexuality. For example, critics of Pope John Paul II's 1993 encyclical letter *Veritatis Splendor* proclaimed that "human sexuality governs this text" (Patrick 1993, 18). Supporters of the encyclical responded that "[f]aith, not sex, is the theme" of the document (Finnis 1994, 69). The apparent goal of the encyclical is to challenge theories of morality held by some Catholic theologians. More specifically, the pope attacks secular trends such as relativism and utilitarianism by explaining and defending more fully the basic principles of Catholic moral theology. He mentions sexuality only a few times, and that in passing. That many understand the real motivation to be uneasiness about sexuality strongly suggests that Catholic discourse about modes of moral reasoning is intricately connected to Catholic sexual teachings; indeed, the responses to *Veritatis Splendor* indicate that the authority of the Church is at stake.

The link between sexual morality and church authority is strong, and it is fortified by Catholic attitudes about order and gender. This book explores those attitudes through a careful study of recent official Catholic documents on sex, marriage, and reproduction. I chose the provocative title *Sexing the Church* because it captures the way Catholicism's attitudes about gender (what it means to be male or female) permeate its teachings about sexuality, reproduction, and church authority. "Sexing" the Catholic Church means revealing the profound interconnection between gender, power, and sexual ethics in the teaching documents of the Church. In recent decades, especially since the Second Vatican Council, sex, gender, and church authority have been among the most controversial issues in Catholicism. Disagreements about contraception, abortion, women in the priesthood, assisted reproductive technologies, and homosexuality all reveal the centrality of Catholicism's understanding of the natural order and its view of authority and obedience. Can the Church change its teachings about morality? Can it abandon traditional ideas about gender roles and sex without severely compromising Catholic beliefs? Catholics believe that the Church's role is to interpret and maintain the natural order of God's creation, an order that relies on the correct interpretation of the meanings of human sexuality and gender. In what follows, I will utilize the concept of order as the organizing metaphor for clarifying Catholic sexual ethics.[2]

In brief, this book explores the notion of order through a significant body of religious writing on morality. The chapters are structured around three concerns: 1) order as reflected in the theology of marriage; 2) the challenge to that order in the second half of the twentieth century through the debates on contraception and assisted reproduction; and 3) the way attitudes about gender in Catholicism connect theological and moral order with ecclesiastical order.

Catholic theology has long exhibited a concern with human sexuality and its relationship to theology and church authority. St. Augustine, for one, made sexuality central to his theology by linking original sin to concupiscence (immoderate desires). In his view, original sin, disobedience, sexual intercourse, and the need for authority were all connected. Augustine claimed that Adam and Eve's original sin was disobedience resulting from pride. They turned away from God, who is the telos of the human striving for the good. Augustine described the disobedience as "this wicked desire which prompts man [*sic*] to please himself as if he were himself light, and which thus turns him away from that light by which, had he followed it, he would have himself become light" (St. Augustine bk. 14, ch. 13). Concupiscence was both evidence of and punishment for original sin: "What but disobedience was the punishment of disobedience in that sin?" (bk. 14, ch. 15). While the term "concupiscence" refers to all immoderate or uncontrolled desires, for Augustine, sexual desires were the most significant because the first effect of Adam and Eve's disobedient act was the awakening of the sexual organs.[3] After the Fall, Adam and Eve "experience a new motion of their flesh, which had become disobedient to them, in strict retribution of their own disobedience to God," writes Augustine (bk. 13, ch. 13).

Hence, to understand the human relationship to God, one needs to grasp the connection between human sexuality and disobedience. Yet sex is necessary to propagate the species and to create families. For Augustine, families are necessary to teach and enforce morality. The husband, on behalf of his wife and children, tries to follow the precepts of morality: to injure no one and to do good to every one he can reach (bk. 19, ch. 14). He is entrusted with the care of his family, and in return the family is duty bound to obey him. For Augustine, family harmony or domestic peace was based on obedience to authority. It flowed from his well-known phrase "The peace of all things is the tranquility of order" (St. Augustine bk. 19, ch. 13). Each thing has its own place. The hierarchy of the family is a check on the human propensity for disobedience; it is the foundational unit of order.

Augustine and the tradition that followed him stressed this inextricable link between theological beliefs, sexual morality, and "the tranquility of order." In this tradition, original sin always mars the human response to God as well as human responses to fellow humans. As a result, the Church guides and directs Catholics in the life of virtue. The Catholic Church understands its role both as interpreting right order (describing the relationship of order to purpose) and as giving orders (regulating and enforcing). This twofold sense of order as created and enforced captures interesting patterns of thought in

Catholic sexual ethics, especially in recent documents on sex, marriage, and reproduction. These documents interpret what God intends for the human sexual act and they also prescribe specific action guides (norms of behavior).

These two senses of order are not merely a matter of individual behavior, they are also a communal matter. And it is at that communal level that religions promulgate and enforce the moral order. This is similar to what David Little describes as society's "process of arranging itself in such a way that its institutional structures and its patterns of authority fit into an ultimate frame of meaning that commands the loyalty of its members" (Little 1969, 7). Marriage is an important example of that societal self-arrangement, and for Catholic teaching, marriage is coherent only when it exists according to an "ultimate frame of meaning"—God. Through marriage, sexual acts are oriented to their proper end, which is the propagation and education of offspring. The Church exercises its authority by teaching the faithful about the proper use and order of sexual faculties. The theology of marriage, the ethics of reproduction, Catholic ecclesiology, and attitudes about gender are all part of the process of arrangement and order characteristic of religion. This process is simply a way to define appropriate relationships, such as the right relationship of humans to God and to each other.

While I want to suggest that viewing this set of Catholic documents through the category of order is helpful, a further purpose of this project is to explore how gender roles permeate these senses of order. Before the Second Vatican Council, Catholic theology claimed that women were subordinate to men. As Pius XI stated, "For if the man is the head, the woman is the heart, and as he occupies the chief place in ruling, so she may and ought to claim for herself the chief place in love" (Pius XI 1930, 15). In the post–Vatican II period, the Church has downplayed the emphasis on subordination of women, as seen in this passage from John Paul II: "[B]oth man and woman are human beings to an equal degree, both are created in God's image" (John Paul II 1988, 6).[4] Hence, while the magisterium continues to emphasize gender difference, they embrace a rhetoric of equality between male and female.[5] Male and female are equal in dignity and equal in God's eyes, but he ordered them to be in relation to each other—a relation that requires difference.

In the arena of sexual relations, equality and difference take on even greater significance, as seen in the renewed emphasis on difference in John Paul II's theology of the body. A human being's gendered identity (understood either in its biological or psychosocial manifestations), while not relevant to God's relationship to the person, is important to sexual identity and practice. There is evidence, then, of both an egalitarian trend (men and women are equal in their dignity) and a subordinating one (men and women each have distinct roles).

Similarly, Catholic attitudes about women in the priesthood also display this contradiction between egalitarian and subordinationist views. As the feminist theologian Rosemary Radford Ruether describes it, "[W]omen are said to be equal in the created order and hence in secular society but subordinate in the redemptive 'mystery' that connects Christ with the eucharistic priesthood" (Ruether 1991, 98). The nature of the equality in the created order is clearly anthropological, but Ruether's point is that the grounds for excluding women from the priesthood suggest an inequality in the redemptive order. Male and female as sexual beings are part of the created order, different yet equal before God. Women are denied access to the "eucharistic" priesthood because allowing them in would upset the redemptive order. Why is it, then, that imagery from the created order (women as mothers, brides, virgins) is often used to describe the redemptive "mystery" that connects Christ with the Church? Why is the Church "sexed" female?

This practice of "sexing" the Church is another way that gendered roles enforce order. Most notably, the Church is sexed female in the common practice of referring to the Church as mother, bride, and virgin. This association of female sexual roles with an institutional entity such as the Church sheds light in two directions. First, it tells us more about how Catholicism understands "the Church." Second, we learn more about how Catholics view the roles of mother, bride, and virgin. This sexing of the Church is more than just an example of how gender and order work in Catholic morality; it also reveals tensions in the complex patterns of Catholic reasoning about marriage, reproduction, and church authority. In a surprising way, it challenges the order enforced by the Catholic ethics of marriage and reproduction.

The concern for alignment and order evident in official Catholic teachings on marriage, reproduction, and gender is structurally similar to attitudes about church authority. In the documents I study, marriage mirrors the properly ordered relationship of God to humans. It also sacralizes the natural teleological order that connects human sexual acts to creation. Moreover, Catholicism's insistence on "chaste marriage" emphasizes the necessary order of a person's passions to her will. These three dimensions—the vertical, horizontal, and internal—are present in various ways through all the texts I consulted for this project. Beginning with Leo XIII's encyclical on marriage in 1880, the magisterium has continuously revisited the matter of how marriage structures, legitimizes, and maintains order. It has been concerned with how to restore order to the temporal realm—an order that, according to Pius XI, is "frustrated and trampled upon by the passions, errors and vices of man [*sic*]" (Pius XI 1930, 49). In Catholicism, the rightly ordered marriage, as we shall see in the next chapter, has profound implications for all created order, especially the alignment of the individual to God, the individual to the neighbor in society, and the components of the individual's soul.

ORDER, RELIGION, AND MORALITY

Before proceeding, however, we must be clear about how and why the category of order is used in this study. The two senses of order, as descriptive of an organized or structured pattern and as a command, help organize and explain Catholic sexual ethics. The first sense captures the Catholic belief about the inherent purposiveness of God's creation, which informs the human understanding of moral action. By contrast, order in the sense of command reflects the emphasis on governance and regulation. Put more succinctly, God has created an order, humans strive to respect and fulfill it, and the Church assists humans by enforcing the appropriate moral norms.

The concept of order is used in theological and philosophical discourse in a variety of ways. The term, understood in its broadest sense, refers to "a structured state of affairs" (Childress 1986, 439). The notion of structure implies a pattern made up of different elements that all relate to each other in some fashion. Order describes the state of that relationship. Thus, a set of elements whose relationship to each other is coherent is said to be in order. Various elements whose relationship is unclear or even antagonistic are often thought to be in disorder. For instance, we use the phrase "out of order" to mean broken or not functioning—not able to achieve its intended purpose.

We might ask, then, what constitutes an ordered state? Often what appears to be utterly disordered (e.g., a messy desk, an abstract painting) may in fact be very much in order. The relationship of the various parts may be systematic, at least in one individual's view. This sort of reflection about the concept of order is relevant to many areas of life; politics, law, art, music, landscape design, physics, and so forth. In the area of theology, the concept of order is important because it describes what believers perceive as the proper state of relationship in the created universe. Indeed, for Christians it illuminates the nature of God's relationship to humans, relationships among humans, and the relationship of the parts of the individual to each other. Catholic sexual ethics invokes all three of these types of order, and they all adhere to a teleological logic, which views order as inseparable from purpose.

John Mahoney's Augustinian description of order captures these three dimensions—vertical, horizontal, and interior. He writes,

> *All the things which God has created are good, and so the rational soul acts well with reference to them if it maintains order, and if by distinguishing, choosing, and assessing, it subordinates the lesser things to the greater, the bodily to the spiritual, the lower to the higher, and the temporal to the eternal. (Mahoney 1987, 75)*

The moral life, then, is about maintaining the order of God's creation as it is manifested in various dimensions. Mahoney summarizes Augustine's ethics in the phrase "a place for everything and everything in its place" (75).[6] Seen through the feminine metaphors for the Church, the Catholic construction of gender reinforces all three of these orders—the feminine has historically been associated with the lesser, the bodily, the lower, and the temporal. Nevertheless, the activity of sexing the Church as feminine undermines that order by presenting a vision that is discontinuous with the reality of church authority as male. In other words, what is the right relationship of the feminine to church authority and rule? Thus, even as the Church sees gender roles as embodiments of God's order, the sexing of the Church as female might suggest some ambiguity in that order.

Charles Curran clarifies contemporary discussions of the Church by noting two distinguishing characteristics of Catholic ecclesiology:

its emphasis on mediation and its hierarchical structure. Mediation, which Curran refers to as "sacramentality" or "analogical imagination," captures the Catholic view that "the divine is mediated in and through the human and the natural."[7] Catholics are confident that the order of nature (God's creation) reveals the divine. The Church is the visible sign of the divine working through the human. The Church is neither fully human nor fully divine, according to this view. Rather, it is a unity; a marriage. In a certain sense, the fruits of that union are the sacraments. They "illustrate the reality of mediation" (Curran 1999, 10). While Curran presents mediation as characteristic of Catholic ecclesiology, he is also critical of historical moments when mediation has led to the claim that the Church is divine, and therefore perfect and sinless.

Curran commends the view adopted by Vatican II of the Church as the pilgrim people of God. This "notion that the church itself is continually growing and developing to overcome its own sinfulness" is truer to the authentic mediating quality of the Church, writes Curran (1999, 13). Describing the Church as the union of the human and the divine has profound implications for how church authority is structured mainly because the Catholic Church is also hierarchical; popes and bishops have authority over a wide range of matters. Curran notes that the Vatican II conception of the pilgrim church provides a significant corrective to the present construction of teaching authority, which concentrates the power with the popes and bishops, especially in matters of morality.

In essence, these two characteristics (mediation and hierarchy) exist in a state of tension. And the nature of that tension helps illuminate the complexities of Catholic sexual ethics. The sacrament of marriage is both symbolic of the Church's unity with God and the fruit of that union. It orders the sexual relationship of male to female in a way that emphasizes both mediation and hierarchy. Indeed, a problem that haunts the twentieth-century literature on marriage and reproduction is how to achieve mediation or equality between the poles of the dualities that have always defined these issues. The construction pleasure *or* procreation struggles with an alternative one—pleasure *and* procreation. Similarly, the hierarchy of male *over* female has been reconfigured in the doctrine of gender complementarity to look like male *and* female. Hence the concurrent struggles: What does it mean to be the Church? Is procreation the only good of sexual union? How does one define gender equality within a scheme that views gender as flowing naturally from biological sex?

GENDER, MARRIAGE, AND REPRODUCTION

The claim that the ethics of marriage and reproduction reflect attitudes about gender is not a new one; both the history of Catholic theology and contemporary church teachings are rife with evidence that supports such a view. Attitudes about gender—by "gender" I mean the practical and theological consequences of having the cultural identity male or female—are a central part of teachings about sex, marriage, and reproduction. The moral systems designed by societies to regulate sexual behavior draw our attention to both the cultural meanings and the biological realities of gender difference.[8]

Most will agree that theories about gender identity are bound up with moral norms governing marriage and reproduction. More controversial is the precise nature of this relationship. What does it mean to say that the ethics of marriage and reproduction reflect attitudes about gender? Is this a statement about causality? Does it suggest an explicit plan to dominate and subjugate women? Or is the interrelation of marriage, reproduction, and gender the natural outcome of a religious tradition that has consistently assigned powerful roles to men? These are significant questions; however, answering them is not the primary goal of this project. While I believe that the norms governing sexual morality bolster gender attitudes as well as reflect them, I am not interested in probing the question of causality. Others have written about the sources of patriarchy and gender injustice in Christianity.[9]

This volume is sympathetic to concerns about unjust gender arrangements in Catholic moral theology and ecclesiology. Indeed, these concerns motivate it to a large extent. However, it differs from the work of feminist theologians and critics in some significant ways. It is not a normative or constructive work of moral theology. Rather, it analyzes and assesses the way a particular religious tradition expresses its morality through various concepts of order and how attitudes about gender permeate and destabilize these concepts. More explicitly, I argue that the doctrine of gender complementarity and the practice in official documents of sexing the Church as feminine present disruptive currents in an otherwise tightly ordered vision of sex, marriage, and reproduction that presupposes a rigid gender scheme. Indeed, what is disrupted is the premise that female sexuality in the context of marriage and reproduction is always submissive or at least is never imbued with authority and is only rarely imbued with agency. Calling the Church "mother," "bride," and "virgin" does not negate the gender inequities found in the Catholic hierarchy, but it certainly does complicate them, especially in the area of reproduction.

GENDER AND METAPHORS

The moral arguments that govern sexual and reproductive behavior are based on unspoken presumptions about male and female roles, a point that is not always explicit in writings on these matters. For instance, the argument from *Humanae Vitae,* Pope Paul VI's encyclical on contraception, that acts which threaten "the inseparable connection between the two meanings of the conjugal act (the unitive and the procreative)" are illicit suggests that procreation is central and must be regulated. On this view, women's roles are defined in relation to maternity, which in essence limits their sphere of influence. The metaphorical description of the Church as mother, for example, transfers maternity, a role usually limited to the private domestic sphere, into the public domain of institutional church structure. Thus, the order that Catholic teaching on marriage and reproduction imposes on gender roles looks different through the lens of these images.

In terminology familiar to feminist theorists, maternal and sexual roles dwell in the sphere of the private. Appropriating them metaphorically to describe a public institution such as the Church transgresses the private/public boundary. By relying on this set of images to describe the public institution of the Church, the gender-specific roles gain a different potency. The atmosphere created by these metaphors presents a more complex and ambiguous view of gender roles than that reflected by the normative moral arguments. Indeed, it is difficult to ignore a practice that sexes the Church female when the church hierarchy is decidedly male. It seems evident that the Church is called female as a way to complement the relationship with a male God/Christ. Hence, its feminine roles are all ones that suggest a relationship to a male: mother of Christ, wife of Christ, body of Christ. It is always in a physical relationship to God, just as women are in physical relationships to men; but this relationship is desexualized because ultimately the Church is always virgin.

The metaphors I explore evoke a set of attitudes about sex, power, and gender. They create an ambiguity between the gendered order of marriage and reproduction and the gendered hierarchy of church governance. I am not suggesting that the authors of Catholic teaching intend this result when they invoke the metaphors. However, one cannot ignore their ubiquity. In one sense, the female images of the Church do reinforce the order of Catholic sexual ethics: mothers, brides, and virgins are depicted in submissive relations to God and the male Christ. The Church is the feminine element that completes the order of creation as male and female.

Another more practical ambiguity emerges from this metaphoric appropriation of female roles. Catholic teaching consistently proclaims that procreation is the natural end of sexual activity and hence a central component of marriage. This leads Catholics to desire this goal perhaps even more intensely than non-Catholics.[10] Infertile married couples are left in a difficult position, especially in the contemporary context of readily available assistance in achieving a pregnancy—assistance that official Catholic teaching prohibits.[11] Hence, the emphasis on reproduction is ambiguous—reproduction is not an absolute good.

Other oppositional pairs such as culture/nature, reason/emotion, and public/private also reflect the order of male to female. The metaphors reveal three themes that reflect a concern for order between the elements of these pairs. The first theme is power, particularly in the context of the Church as an institutional structure. While the metaphors I study all depict women in a stance of submission, the metaphoric association with the Church raises questions about women's authority. Furthermore, while these gendered metaphors are often used to prescribe obedience, it is an obedience that church documents describe as ultimately leading to freedom. Power is an important consideration when analyzing Catholic teachings about sexuality, since the teachings emerge from a hierarchical power structure. Thus, the norms related to marriage and reproduction carry an authoritative force; the Church regulates sexual activity and its consequences.[12] The notion that sex and power are intimately linked supports my contention about the centrality of "right" order in Catholic sexual ethics.

The second theme concerns sexuality and its valuation. Sexuality is part of all three images captured in the roles of mother, virgin, and spouse, but each role contains conflicts. Sex is good, especially when directed to the end of procreation, but it also must be controlled. Thus, Catholic teaching encourages marital intercourse and conjugal chastity. The ideal sexual relation between husband and wife is ultimately an experience of self-mastery. The construction of Mary, as well as representations of the images of mother and bride, best display this dualism between sexuality and chastity. This theme correlates to Catholic concerns about the relationship of the natural order to the supernatural; to claim that sexual intercourse is a good implies a broad range of theological presuppositions.

These metaphors share a third important theme—gender role and location. The gender-complementarity model reinforces the public/private dichotomy that has so often been grafted to the male/female distinction. It designates to women a particular role in the family. All the metaphors rely on women's roles as mothers and caretakers of the domestic sphere. The central rupture to the order between spheres occurs when the Church is described as mother. The Church, a hierarchy based on patriarchal principles, is clearly a public institution very much unlike a mother.

The intersection of power, sexuality, and gender roles is a focus of interest in religion and gender studies. More precisely, this intersection can wreak havoc on perceived notions of the separation of the public and the private spheres. All three of these categories transgress the boundary between the public and private, particularly when they are placed in relation to each other. Notions of justice and equality, which are usually associated with the public, political realm, have clear private implications. Regulating sexual activity and defining gender roles are both practices that involve an exercise of power over private activities. Furthermore, history has shown that control of women's sexuality, or even anxiety about it, is connected to women's oppression.[13]

Caroline Walker Bynum discusses what it means to analyze gender-related symbols. Her discussion stems from the belief that 1) all human beings are gendered and that gender is culturally constructed, and 2) religious symbols "have the quality of possessing manifold meanings." Hence she writes,

> [G]ender-related symbols . . . do not simply determine the self-awareness of men and women as gendered nor do they simply reflect cultural assumptions about what it is to be male or female. Gender-related symbols, in their full complexity, may refer to gender in ways that affirm or reverse it, support or question it; or they may, in their basic meaning, have little at all to do with male and female roles. (Bynum 1986, 2)

The last part of Bynum's quote translates quite well to the discussion of order and metaphors in this volume.

SEX AND GENDER: TROUBLED TERMS

I have been using the terms "sex" and "gender" throughout this chapter. Before continuing our discussion, it is important to pause and reflect on their troublesome nature. Definitions of these terms are notoriously difficult to determine because they presuppose particular theories of gender and sex. For the purpose of this project, I use them to mean what I think the documents intend by them; for the most part, Catholic documents use them interchangeably because from the Catholic perspective, both biological sex and gendered attributes are natural, not socially constructed. Hence, these official documents do not consider debates about the difference between sex and gender or the relationship of sex and gender to each other to be especially relevant. For the purposes of this analysis, however, it is necessary at least to note the various controversies surrounding these terms. I have organized these controversies into five general questions.

First is the very plausibility of the sex/gender dichotomy. Do sex and gender represent two different aspects of identity? Or are they merely synonymous terms? It has become quite common to view the term "sex" as descriptive of biological traits and "gender" as descriptive of the cultural meanings we assign to sex. Hence, sex is often described as a naturally occurring fact, while gender is viewed as a culturally constructed concept. While defining these two terms differently helps draw attention to an important observation about the context-dependent nature of gender construction, it can pose a significant theological problem for Catholics; it challenges the natural givenness of God's creation of humans as male and female.

A second point of controversy concerns exactly what it means to say that gender is culturally constructed. For instance, does it mean that gender does not have any natural connection to sex so that a biological male could have a female gender, or vice versa? Or could it also mean that what is cultural about gender is that it is an outward expression of our physically inscribed sex? Gender is cultural in the sense that male and female could exhibit different customs or habits in different cultural contexts. But biological sexual characteristics continue to be the primary markers of gender identity in Western societies. Judith Butler claims that both sex and gender are culturally constructed—essentially that neither can be described as natural or prediscursive (existing before language) (Butler 1990, 6–7). Thus we can see that even among those who view gender and sex as representing two different aspects of the human person, there is wide disagreement about what it means to hold that view.

A third debate involves the binary construction of both terms. In the cases of sex and gender, there are only two culturally sanctioned options—male and female. Why? Butler raises this question in speaking of the identity of what she calls "incoherent" or "discontinuous" gendered beings. These persons fail to conform to "the gendered norms of intelligibility by which persons are defined" (Butler 1990, 17). Put more directly, why only two sexes and genders?

A fourth set of questions concerns the relationship of sex and gender to each other. Must they mimic each other? In other words, if individuals "construct" identities, why must there be correlations between male sex and male gender or between female sex and female gender? Those who challenge the rigid correlation between sex and gender generally believe that the relationship between biological sex and the performance of gender identity is a construction. Like the previous debate, some believe that keeping sex and gender in such a proximate relation limits the possibilities available for humans to flourish.

A fifth area of debate pertains to the nature of both terms. In Butler's language, do people have genders, or are they genders? This ontological question is really about whether gender is an identity that is deeply seated in the essence of the person. Some, like Butler, claim that it is an activity or performance and that it forms one's identity only to the extent that identity itself is a practice rather than a preexisting marker of subjectivity. In the fourth chapter of the book, I will revisit some of these difficult questions about gender and sex, especially as they relate to the Catholic doctrine of gender complementarity.

RECENT CATHOLIC DISCUSSIONS OF SEX AND GENDER

Two recent books by Lisa Cahill and Mark Jordan on religion, sex, and gender provide revealing examples of the centrality of the debates described above. While both authors are associated primarily with the Catholic tradition, their works appeal to a wider audience. In both cases, the authors refer to their view of the relation of sex and gender, but neither devotes much space to exploring the issue. What is interesting for our purposes is the contrasting way they view gender and what that contrast means for their normative ethic of sexuality.

Cahill's project is to come up with a language about sex and family that resonates universally while advancing a feminist perspective which she defines as "a commitment to equal personal respect and equal social power for women and men" (Cahill 1996, 1). She embraces the Aristotelian-Thomistic tradition's confidence in the possibility of "shared moral values, at least at a fundamental and general level" (2). These values are to be more than abstractions; they constitute "broad areas of agreement about human needs, goods, and fulfillments which can be reached inductively and dialogically through human experience" (2). She grounds her desire for a universally coherent language in what she calls "the basic human experience of being a self" (2). For Cahill, gender is part of that experience, and while she assumes "cross-cultural differentiation of the human body into male and female sexes which cooperate for reproduction," she rejects its use in the establishment of unjust hierarchical arrangements (82).

Cahill tries to avoid the theoretical morass surrounding the category of gender by accepting that it is informed both by biological and cultural meanings. Furthermore, while she rejects gender as the central category of identity, she holds that one's gender, especially as experienced through sex and reproduction, does affect identity. Thus, instead of viewing gender as a category that limits human possibilities, she describes it as a "moral project" that enhances opportunity. Gender, for Cahill, describes the way men and women transform their biological differences, as well as their capacities, into meaningful and just social relations. Cahill is aware that gender hierarchies often result from gender differentiation and reciprocity. In a later work, she describes the process by which basic biological differences are extended to distinct gender roles whereby women are assigned to "less-valued roles" that are reinforced "by ideology and by physical force, both direct and indirect." Gender hierarchies lead to the exclusion of women and girls from "social authority, power, and even material goods—another contradiction of the inclusive eschatological community symbolized by Jesus' preaching of the reign of God" (Cahill 2000, 50).

Like Cahill, Mark Jordan sidesteps many of the debates about whether gender is a meaningful or an oppressive category. However, he does this in a slightly different way. Whereas Cahill attempts to rehabilitate gender and mold it to her larger normative project of devising an adequate Christian sex ethic, Jordan tries as much as possible to keep a distance between an ethics of sex and an ethics of gender. Jordan acknowledges the profound indeterminacy of both gender and sex—a position quite distinct from Cahill's. Cahill has more at stake in retaining the stability of these categories, since her goal is to support a family-centered, heterosexual sex ethic. Jordan's project has a different goal altogether. It is to devise a sex ethic founded on erotic pleasure, particularly its capacity to enable new roles and identities that transcend dichotomies and obsessions with "fixed sex-identities" (Jordan 2002, 172).

Jordan's study of Christian sexual ethics is a study of "genital acts" and the way these acts contribute to states, statuses, and identities. His focus on acts is especially striking in an environment that valorizes the agent/subject. But he argues that acts provide a good starting point because to speak of acts immediately invokes circumstances, and the moral valuation of sexual acts has always concerned judgments about acceptable circumstances. Thus, Jordan's focus on acts is a bit misleading. Indeed, he is more interested in the contexts of acts and in the way acts form identities and statuses.

On this point, I follow Jordan's helpful suggestion that "we should avoid simply equating an ethics of sex with an ethics of gender." For Jordan, "Sex is not something that happens only 'between the sexes.' Nor are sexual states, statuses and identities simply reducible to the prevailing gender scheme in a society" (16). Like Jordan, I reject the view that discourses about sex and about gender are reducible one to the other. I also support the notion that the precise nature of the relationship is difficult to capture because, in Jordan's words, "the two discourses unroll through, over, against one another" (17).

Both Cahill and Jordan turn to resources in the Catholic tradition to support their normative projects. Cahill retains the categories of gender and sex and believes that justice and equality can be achieved at the same time that difference is valued. Jordan's approach is more focused and radical. He asks that a new Christian ethic (theology) of sex "project alternate identities in which the capacity for erotic pleasure was integrated rather than rejected" (Jordan 2002, 170). Both Cahill and Jordan show, albeit in different ways, the complexity of the categories sex and gender.

STRUCTURE OF THE BOOK

Following this introductory chapter, I divide the book into three segments. Chapter 2 explores three themes in the twentieth-century Catholic theology of marriage: sacramentality, procreation, and chastity. All three of these themes reflect the concern for order that prevails throughout the tradition. Sacramentality focuses on the vertical relationship of God and humans; procreation on the teleological order of the natural world; and chastity on the internal order of the person's will. The task of describing the proper purpose of sexual acts is central in this literature. In this view, sexual intercourse is only licit when the participants understand their place in relation to God. It is a relationship that makes moral sense of the natural order. Thus, the morality of sex is evident in the very structure of the physical act—a structure that is decidedly teleological. The married couple must see their sexual acts as part of the larger context of their relationship to God and their relationship to the natural world. However, because of the human state of sin, the struggle entailed by the proper ordering of sexuality is perhaps most severe at the internal level. Sexual self-control (chastity) is required to affirm the authenticity of the individual's intention both toward God and toward neighbor.

Chapter 3 evaluates the ethics of reproductive control, focusing on artificial contraception and assisted reproductive technologies. First, I situate the debates about these issues in the context of the crisis in authority precipitated by the Second Vatican Council in the 1960s. I then isolate three arguments that characterize the Church's moral teaching on reproduction. The first concerns the morality of actions: the object, intention, and circumstances of an action must be in proper alignment. The second element is the emphasis on the "inseparable connection" between the two meanings of the sexual act. The third is the principle of totality—a principle that is invoked in different ways by opponents in the debate. All three of these arguments rest on the notions of alignment and the ordering of parts to the whole.

There are obvious overlaps between the Church's arguments on contraception and on reproductive technology. First, they both concern active involvement in the processes of generation—one by impeding the process and the other by facilitating it. Second, they both reflect the perennial tension in Christian ethics between procreation and pleasure as legitimate goals of sexual relations. Finally, while the emphasis on the inseparability of the meanings was first offered as part of the argument against most forms of contraception, it has appeared more recently in arguments against assisted reproductive technologies. It is interesting to note that if the Church had maintained its insistence on procreation as *the* primary end, it might have been more difficult to make the argument against technological assistance that facilitates the achievement of that end.

In chapter 4, I explore more carefully how attitudes about gender, especially when expressed in the metaphors that describe the Church as feminine, connect theological and moral order with ecclesiastical order. I begin with gender complementarity and note interesting similarities between this doctrine and the argument about the inseparability of the meanings of sexual acts. I then explore metaphors that describe the Church as feminine, focusing especially on maternal metaphors. I extend this analysis from the realm of sexual ethics to moral theology in general by claiming that the metaphors create an atmosphere of instability about the appropriate role of women that leads to confusion and ambiguity about women's authority and agency.

These metaphors are relevant to Catholic sexual morality because they embody and convey Catholic views about sex and gender in a different way than do the official teaching documents. This in itself is not a new insight, but I want to highlight the tensions between the images and the actual teachings. In other words, I want to suggest that rather than reinforcing church teachings, these metaphors often undermine them. For instance, Susan Ross argues that while the nuptial metaphor has been used extensively in the Christian spiritual and mystical traditions in ways that were not intended to prescribe gender roles, the more contemporary usage of this metaphor "consciously and purposefully" prescribes such roles. She also illustrates how this metaphor, especially in the theology of John Paul II, emerges from "an aesthetic and typological interpretation of the Bible that itself already assumes gender complementarity" (Ross 2001, 41). Ross's assessment of this metaphor is decidedly negative. She suggests that the description of God's relationship to humanity in nuptial terms simply highlights the asymmetry of power between God and humans. I think Ross's assessment about the power relation implied by the metaphor is correct, but I want to press the analysis to reveal further ambiguity in the metaphor.[14]

While the subject matter of this study is the Catholic Church, the mode of reading and evaluating texts as well as the conclusions I reach about marriage, reproduction, gender, and church authority is relevant to the study of any religious tradition. Indeed, one can configure the relationship of gender, sex, and authority in various ways. In an essay on love, sex, and gender in Haitian Vodou, Elizabeth McAlister describes her methodology as seeking "to examine the complex relationship of religion to the construction of love, gender, and sexuality." She notes that while the academic study of the construction and interaction of class, race, gender, and sexuality has thrived in recent years, religion has rarely been taken into account. This, she notes, is ironic since "religious systems are in the business of constructing the world and then naturalizing its meaning as "true" (McAlister 2000, 130). For McAlister, religion plays a crucial role in organizing society and in authorizing truth claims. Central to that organizing task is religious discourse on marriage and sex. Hence, we must pay attention to its relationship to the construction of love, gender, and sexuality.

Throughout this study, I read official texts with an eye to the linguistic nuances they present. I am interested in imagery and metaphor; this volume is structured around the images of order and alignment. Love, gender, and sexuality are all construed by Catholic theology in terms of order. Love is teleological in orientation with God as the ultimate telos. Gender is the most primeval mark of human creature-liness. Thus, not only does Catholicism order the male to the female, but humans are thought to display the proper alignment of the human to the divine by fulfilling their gendered roles. Catholic documents view the relationship of male to female in all facets of life as an extension of God's divine plan—it orders human sexuality and reproduction. For Catholicism, this set of ordered relationships is solidified by the sacrament of marriage, making all these activities religious at their very core.

THEOLOGY AND MARRIAGE

2

Whatever things have deviated from their right order, cannot be back to that original state which is in harmony with their nature except by a return to the divine plan which, as the Angelic Doctor teaches, is the exemplar of all right order.

—Pius XI 1930, 49

Sex for procreation is good; sexual passions are unruly; marriage is a sacrament. The values embedded in these three statements are not just expressions of Catholic sexual ethics; they reflect the core of Catholic theological beliefs about nature, creation, grace, and sin. Consequently, to better answer the question How does the concept of order clarify Catholic views about gender, sexual ethics, and Church authority? we must probe Catholicism's core theological claims. Put more directly, the interconnections between theology and sexual norms are too central to ignore. Catholic claims about the purposes of sexual intercourse and the place of sexual activity in the context of the God/human relationship rest upon as well as reinforce a particular view of what it means to be male or female in the context of God's created order. Marriage, as the legitimate locus of sexual intercourse, institutionalizes those gender roles and attitudes. There is an order to sexual activity and, more generally, to the male/female relationship that is ultimately connected to the properly ordered relationship between God and creation. In Catholicism, marriage has traditionally played an important role in enacting that order.

Views about procreation and gender are central components of Catholicism's precise and well-developed theology of marriage. It is a theology grounded in an understanding of marriage as mirroring the covenant of God and his people, especially as exemplified by the "marriage of Christ and the Church." Like the covenant between God and the people of Israel and God's gift of his son, marriage is, in the words of Paul VI in *Humanae Vitae,* "the wise institution of the Creator to realize in mankind His design of love." Marriage is not "the effect of chance or the product of evolution of unconscious natural forces" but rather a deliberate part of God's created order (Paul VI 1968, par. 8). The view that marriage reflects an essential component of God's relationship to humans grounds the normative claims of Catholic sexual ethics.

In this chapter, I identify three basic assertions about the connection between marriage, the created order, and God: 1) the primary meaning of marriage is sacramental; 2) the primary end of marriage is procreation; and 3) the primary virtue in marriage is chastity. These assertions reflect a theological order, one that entails a certain relationship between male and female. The institution of marriage and gender roles reinforce one another and work to maintain what Catholicism views as God's created order. This chapter underscores the ways the concept of marriage as a sacrament captures the vertical dimension of that order; the ways the teleological language of ends captures the social dimension of that order; and the ways the virtue of chastity focuses on the agent and the importance of self-mastery in maintaining that order.

References to the meaning, end, and virtue of marriage reflect views about sexual activity in marriage. The documents and themes I explore in this chapter all exhibit a concern about how to justify sexual intercourse and, more precisely, how to legitimize its pleasure. As noted earlier, concupiscence or immoderate desire is both a sign of and a punishment for a disordered self. Defining what constitutes moderate or appropriate desire is a central task for these documents that has implications for all three types of order mentioned above—the vertical dimension, the social dimension, and the agent-centered dimension. The line between legitimate sexual pleasure and "unbridled lust" is thus a fine one in these documents. Nevertheless, the most significant developments in the contemporary period, which begins with Leo XIII's 1880 encyclical letter on marriage, are the shift in the construal of sexual pleasure and the implications of that shift for the meaning of procreation.

Leo's document is in some ways an arbitrary starting point since it is preceded by a rich history of Catholic theological reflection on sex and marriage.[1] It does, however, represent the start of more-sustained and systematic magisterial reflection on these issues, especially as responses to fast-paced societal changes.[2] In his 1965 book on the history and development of Catholic views on contraception, John Noonan presents a thorough account of the tensions and reactions that have formed Church teachings on sex and marriage. His study traces this history up to the Vatican II period. Noonan, writing as part of the 1960s conversation about the morality of contraception, argues that the Catholic view of sexuality and marriage must be seen as the development of a doctrine.[3] He evokes another image about the Catholic doctrine on sexuality, claiming that it is "not the logical projection of a single value, but a balance of a whole set of competing values" (Noonan 1965, 300). These values include the goodness of procreation, the superiority of virginity, and the institutional value of marriage.

Noonan's metaphor of a balance of values to describe the development of church teaching on sexual morality is controversial within Catholic circles because it implies that one value may be sacrificed for the sake of another, an image that contradicts the Catholic view that moral teachings are stable and not open to development. However, in the context of this study's emphasis on order, balancing represents the type of egalitarian order (e.g., a move away from a hierarchical order between husband and wife and between the ends of marriage) promoted by recent Catholic documents on marriage and reproduction. Consequently, I find Noonan's claims about viewing church doctrine on sexuality as a development impelled by attempts to balance competing values accurate and in tune with recent Catholic thought. In that spirit, then, I explore these values as they appear in the major church statements on marriage from the papacy of Leo XIII to the present.

SACRAMENT

The belief that marriage is a sacrament informs all Catholic discourse about marriage. More precisely, the sacramental nature of marriage both explains and justifies the construction of chastity and procreation in Catholic doctrine. St. Augustine includes sacrament (along

23

with children and fidelity) as one of the three ends of marriage. The view of marriage as sacrament also reveals the connection of marriage to the broader theological scheme of Catholicism. Unlike the other two ends, which follow from principles of natural law, "the end of sacrament is a graced state" (Hogan 1993, 16). John Paul II depicts sacraments as a way to make the faithful witnesses of, as well as sharers in, the salvation event. He claims that every sacrament is "a memorial, actuation and prophecy" (John Paul II 1981, 26). These three terms suggest a temporal succession; memorial captures the past, actuation the present, and prophecy the future. Sacrament as sign and real representation implies a simultaneous looking backward and forward while also actualizing in the present the very meaning of the sacrament. This emphasis on chronological order echoes Catholicism's overall emphasis on ordered relationships.

Using the image of temporal succession, we might ask What does marriage as a sacrament reveal about the past? What does it accomplish in the present? And what does it foretell about the future? For example, some elements of the magisterial discourse focus on the sacrament of marriage as a memorial or commemoration of God's creation of the first couple, Adam and Eve. Other elements, notably witness and hope, look to the future, as does the sacramental end of the "the perfection of the natural love of the spouses and their mutual sanctification" (Hogan 1993, 13). The practice of living out the family relationship in a loving and forgiving manner exemplifies the present actuation of the marital sacrament. John Paul II expresses the temporal aspect of the sacrament in these theological terms. He writes, "As the sacrament of the human beginning, as the sacrament of the temporality of the historical man [sic], marriage fulfills in this way an irreplaceable service in regard to his extra-temporal future, in regard to the mystery of the redemption of the body in the dimension of the eschatological hope" (John Paul II 1997, 351).

John Paul II's description of the temporal dimension of sacraments parallels Susan Ross's identification of the three bases of Christian sacramentality in a fascinating way. They are, according to Ross, "its rootedness in the revelatory character of creation, its communal dimension, and its connection to the life of Jesus the Christ" (Ross 1998, 39).[4] The revelatory character of creation describes the sacrament as memorial; the emphasis on sacrament in community is an aspect of actuation in the present; and the incarnation represents the eschatological hope in the future. Ross also argues that "sacramentality means that created reality *both* reveals *and* conceals the presence of God." For Ross, sacraments display both "an opacity and a transparency" (1998, 39). Thus, she encourages us to explore the ambiguous reality of sacramentality. The theological project of explaining marriage in three temporal supports Ross's contention about this ambiguous reality.

The Sacrament of Marriage as Memorial

The divine origin of marriage, the effect of original sin on marriage, and Christ's role in the restoration of marriage are the most prominent features of the description of marriage as memorial. In *Arcanum Diviniae Sapientiae,* Leo XIII makes explicit the connection between the divine origin of marriage and its significance as a Christian sacrament. The divine origin is also significant because it grants the Church authority over the institution of marriage. Leo's letter is notable because it says little about procreation, pleasure, or chastity, three issues that preoccupy the later magisterial writings on marriage. Instead, in response to the anxiety of that era about the secular regulation of marriage, it emphasizes the origin of marriage and its sacramentality. To identify marriage as holy and as part of God's plan imbues the Church with authority to control and regulate marriage. Grounding the sacrament in the historical event of the marriage of Adam and Eve reminds the faithful that the sacrament both reveals and enacts that history.

Leo XIII describes Adam and Eve's original sin and its effect in the context of Christ's restoration: "[H]e imparted to all things a new form and beauty banishing every trace of age and decay" (Liebard 1978, 1). The ultimate consequence and sign of that decay is increased state control over the institution. As nations lost sight of the origin of marriage, they enacted laws and invented ceremonies to fill the void. Marriage came to be seen as a useful instrument of the state rather than as part of God's will and plan. Leo attributes the origin of marriage to the biblical account of creation. God created Adam and Eve so that they might be the "source of mankind and that from them the human race should be propagated and by uninterrupted course of procreation, be preserved to all time" (2–3). This union between man and woman has ("bears on its face") two essential properties—unity and perpetuity (monogamy and indissolubility).[5] We see once again the powerful temporal sense of the sacrament. Marriage is a process, not a one-time event. Later in the encyclical, Leo adds another item to the list of attributes—sanctity. These three attributes give marriage its "fertile and salutary force." God authorized the Church to regulate the marriages of Christians, and Leo makes clear that this authority is not the result of "the concession of men"; it is an expression of God's will.

Christ's role as the divine restorer is illustrated through the gospel story of the marriage at Cana.[6] His most important contribution to this project of restoration, however, is that he raised marriage to the status of a sacrament by "cementing it more firmly in the bonds of charity." In *Casti Connubii,* Pius XI gives a more direct explanation of Christ's precise task of restoration. It is linked to the fact that "the primeval law" against divorce was loosened by God for Moses and his people "on account of the hardness of their hearts" (Pius XI 1930, 18). In his famous utterance "What God hath joined together let no man put asunder" (Matthew 19:6) Christ effectively restored the integrity of the primeval law.[7] To say that marriage is a sacrament is to say that it is a sacred sign conveying grace. Thus, it signifies the gift of God's love (divine charity), a gift that, in Leo XIII's words, is most evident in "the mystic nuptials of Christ and Church" (Liebard 1978, 12).

The most detailed discussion of the origin of marriage is found in the writing of John Paul II.[8] He characterizes marriage as the "primordial sacrament" and argues that to understand the sacrament of marriage fully, we must situate it as "an integral part" of creation. He reads Genesis 2:24 through the lens of Ephesians 5:21–33 and claims that the Genesis passage, which describes man and woman as becoming one flesh, depicts the original marriage.[9] Furthermore, it is the "beginning of the fundamental human community which through the 'procreative' power that is proper to it serves to continue the work of creation" (John Paul II 1997, 335).

John Paul II premises his discussion of the origin of marriage as sacrament on a strong dichotomy between the natural and the supernatural. Marriage has been a sacrament from the beginning of creation, but it is a natural one in the sense that it serves to justify sexual relations between man and woman. God's revelation of the supernatural order through the gift of his son raised marriage to an institution that signifies as well as conveys grace. As a sacrament of grace, however, marriage is an institution that justifies the relationship before God. Marriage as a natural or primordial sacrament is sufficient to contain the personalistic norm—John Paul II's version of Kant's respect for persons—but it is devoid of "the heritage of original grace" and "supernatural efficacy" because of original sin (1997, 337). The supernatural aspect of the sacrament contains even more; it embraces matrimony as part of God's divine plan of sanctification and redemption.

Drawing our attention to the way marriage as sacrament reveals and affirms God's creative power, these official writings also suggest a defined pattern of gender identity and relationship. This is most obvious in the description of Adam and Eve (male and female) as the "primordial" couple, but it is also evident in the connection between sacrament and procreation as the ends of marriage. Marriage, especially procreation, can sanctify and redeem. Given the prominence of the gendered roles of male and female in sexual intercourse and procreation, that sanctification and redemption is necessarily connected to gender identity. Finally, because marriage is a sacrament that binds man and woman to God, reaffirming the covenantal nature of the relationship elevates the male/female relationship to primary status. It becomes the quintessential human relationship and reduces one's identity within that relationship to gender. As we shall see in chapter 4, the Catholic theory of gender complementarity is intimately connected to the creation story, especially in the theology of John Paul II.

The Sacrament of Marriage as Actuation

In addition to reminding the faithful of the divine origins of marriage, its sacramental quality also draws attention to the present moment. Marriage, when raised to the status of sacrament, achieves three purposes in the present: it protects women, it prohibits divorce, and it justifies the sexual act. According to the official Catholic view, prior to the restoration brought about by Jesus Christ, societies had become utterly confused about marriage. Leo's description of the abuses that resulted is most notable for its attention to the plight of women. According to Leo, one way that marriage serves the "actuating" function is that it protects women. He writes, "There was also a great disturbance of the mutual rights and duties of married persons when the husband acquired dominion over the wife." Leo views marriage as protecting women from male dominion in marriage. He does, however, affirm that the right ordering of the marital relationship requires the wife to submit to the husband: "[T]he man is the chief of the family, and the head of the woman. . . . [She] should be subject to and obey the man, not as servant, but as companion; and so neither honor nor dignity is lost by the rendering of obedience" (Liebard 1978, 6). On this view, the woman's subjection and obedience to the man is an element of the rights and duties that are inherent in the marital relationship. The gender-specific roles receive even greater authority through their connection to the nuptial metaphor of Christ and Church. This metaphor captures the centrality of the power relationship that characterizes marriage. Marriage institutionalized as a sacrament serves several functions; most notably, it enables the Church to claim that the sacramental state protects women and it denies the important function that the state might have in ensuring justice in the domestic sphere.

The second aspect of the sacrament of marriage that focuses on the present is the prohibition against divorce. Because marriage is sacred and part of God's plan, it "bears on its face" the attributes of unity, perpetuity, and sanctity. Leo's encyclical addresses how to reconcile that truth with the secular regulation of marriage. While he does not want to strip states of their power completely, he does want them to realize that "Christian wisdom" is the basis of even these laws of civilization. He urges the state to realize how much it needs the Church's view on this issue—a view that is based on reason and wisdom. Indeed, the practical issue that drives Leo's encyclical is the state's legalization of divorce. He proclaims in no uncertain terms that divorce leads to bad consequences, and he provides an extensive list of them. Leo gives the impression that even the clear violation of the sacramental bond is of less concern than the harm that divorce causes to the self and society.

Several decades later, in *Casti Connubii,* Pius XI argues that the most significant blessing of marriage is its sacramental quality: the sacramental bond assists married couples in living up to the duties of matrimony. He writes, "These parties, let it be noted, not fettered but adorned by the golden bond of the sacrament, not hampered but assisted, should strive with all their might to the end that their wedlock, not only through the power and symbolism of the sacrament, but also through their spirit and manner of life may be and remain always the living image of that most fruitful union of Christ with the Church, which is to be venerated as the sacred token of most perfect love" (Pius XI 1930, 23). Thus, instead of being a burden on married couples, the sacramental nature of marriage helps couples achieve the ideal of "most perfect love."

As is common in most Catholic writing on the topic, Pius XI often describes marriage as sacred or holy. Secular views of marriage make the erroneous claim that marriage is a human invention. Pius XI responds to this error by describing the divine origin of marriage, its purpose of begetting children and binding man and wife, and its nature as a means of transmitting life. He contrasts sacredness with religious character—the religious character of marriage is evident because we know it to be a sublime sign of grace and, in particular, a sign of the union between Christ and Church. Marriage as a sign of the ultimate covenant provides a model against which to judge the marital relationship. In terms of gender roles, it is a model that sets a high standard.

Like Leo, Pius XI addresses the issue of church-state relations as it impinges on marriage, but he focuses on another concern in his encyclical letter—the need to respond to other Christian Churches who appear to be loosening their prohibition on contraception. Hence, procreation is one of the blessings of marriage that concerns its present actuation. More particularly, the supernatural element imbues the nuptial bond through a different understanding of the notion of procreation. What had been seen as the mere propagation of the human race is now seen as the propagation of offspring for the Church. Pius XI states, "Christian parents must also understand that they are destined not only to propagate and preserve the human race on earth"; their role is to propagate and educate children who will become Catholics. This duty stems from the belief that Catholic progeny can only be sanctified when parents "offer their offspring to the Church," who as "the most fruitful mother of the Children of God" is able through baptism to regenerate and sanctify the offspring (9).

The Sacrament of Marriage as Prophecy

The notion of eschatological hope in the "future encounter with Christ" captures the prophetic role of the sacrament of marriage. The image of bearing witness bridges the present practices and virtues necessary for marriage with the future goal. The sacrament not only memorializes the past and regulates the present, it also looks forward to a future union with God. The incarnation animates the prophetic power of the sacrament. The sacrament is a "real representation" of Christ's relationship to the Church.

An address by Pius XII to the World Union of Family Organizations offers one of the most potent discussions of the relationship of marriage and eschatological hope. In speaking to the group about the "spiritual and religious problems of widowhood," Pius XII remarks that widows who choose not to remarry exhibit a devotion and faithfulness unlike that found in those who remarry. Hence, "although the Church does not condemn remarriage, she shows her predilection for souls who wish to remain faithful to their spouse." He bases this claim on his interpretation of the true meaning of the sacrament of marriage as symbolizing the "perfect" union of God and human. Pius XII writes, "[F]ar from destroying the bonds of human and supernatural love which are contracted in marriage, death can perfect them and strengthen them." He argues that while "legally and on the plane of perceptible realities," death brings an end to marriage; there is an eternal aspect of the marriage vows that lives on (Liebard 1978, 193). Just as humans live on eternally as souls, so too should their sacramental bonds.

More practically, he asks the widow to do more than simply refrain from remarriage. She is expected to mirror, as it were, the sacrifice of her husband's death, to accept "the cross of separation." She does this by living a life of prayer, meditation, detachment, and renunciation of "the intense but fleeting joys of sensible and carnal affection" (194). The sacramental grounding of marriage is its real representation of "Christ's redeeming love for the Church." The nuptial metaphor is used to great effect to make this point. The widow is like the Church who has been separated from her spouse (Christ). Just as the Church remains faithful to Christ by waiting hopefully for the "final fulfillment," so too ought the widowed woman understand her vows as eternal, transcending the barriers between this world and the next.

John Paul II expresses the prophetic, future-oriented element of the sacrament of marriage in a slightly different way. For him, the concept of "justice toward the creator" is what ultimately requires that sexual activity between man and woman be made just (justified) in the eyes of God. John Paul II applies his version of the personalistic norm (to never treat the other merely as a means to an end) to the human relationship to God. As creator, God has rights, and humans recognize those rights by obeying the order of nature and by emphasizing the value of the person (John Paul II 1960, 247). In order to be true "co-creators" with God, the married couple must embrace an integrated personalistic love. A central element of that love is openness to parenthood. Such openness guarantees that the sexual act is an expression of true love, not simply "reciprocal sexual exploitation," and through this expression, humans "discharge their duties to the creator" (248–249). Participating in marriage as a sacrament requires openness to procreation. Eschatological hope is expressed through this openness.

PROCREATION

Catholicism has viewed procreation, which in the official documents usually refers to both the propagation and the education of offspring as the primary end or purpose of conjugal sex. The language of ends is by no means alien to Catholicism, a tradition whose logic is markedly teleological. Relying on the Thomistic understanding of human action, the licitness of acts is judged by their orientation toward their proper, intended end. In fact, Catholic moral theology often uses the term "disordered" to describe sinful acts.[10] The notion of a created order as the foundation of moral norms is especially prevalent in Catholic discussions of sexual ethics. The language of ends is often replaced with the language of purposes or, as we shall see in *Casti Connubii,* the language of blessings. Each of the three terms—"end," "purpose," or "blessing"—implies rather different things. All three, however, derive their logic from the view that all sexual acts must have a purpose and that God intended only one. Thus, licit sexual acts are those that cohere with the intended purpose of sex; illicit ones contradict that purpose.

Gareth Moore observes that Catholic documents use the phrase "the purpose of sex" synonymously with "the Creator's design for sex." Purpose is not merely coincidental. According to Moore, the tradition claims that "God's purpose in making us sexual is that we might reproduce" (Moore 1992, 64). Moore, however, argues against the view that assigns purposes to sex. He claims that the tradition perceives purpose and pleasure as a binary opposition. In other words, when the tradition says that the sole justification of sexual intercourse is procreation, it seems to preclude the claim that the pursuit of pleasure through sex is legitimate. Moore offers a helpful distinction between what he calls strong and weak forms of "the procreative purpose theory." The theory, in its most basic form, claims that the purpose of sex is procreation. The strong form, according to Moore, is that procreation is the only justification for sex. Over time, that view was modified (weakened, in Moore's view) to the claim that preventing procreation or performing sexual acts such that children could not result rendered those acts sinful. So in the strong formulation, one should engage in sexual activity only if the intent is procreative. The weak form shifts the focus from simply stating that the purpose of sex is procreative to articulating the boundaries of appropriate sexual behavior. In the weaker form, there is room for other purposes for sex as long as the procreative purpose is not frustrated.

The discussion of marriage as the locus of procreation is relevant to Catholic norms that govern contraception and assisted reproduction. In both cases, the precise view held about the role of procreation in justifying sexual activity is crucial to the development of moral norms. The traditional view about the theology of procreation is, in Eugene Rogers's words, that "human beings are created in God's image in that as God creates, human beings procreate" (Rogers 1999, 204). Hence, human procreation is a way to fulfill the image of God.[11] Moreover, the Church "genders" the activity of reproduction. As we shall see in what follows, for Pius XII, propagation of offspring serves different theological purposes for men than for women. This connects with one of my claims about the effects of gender on issues of reproduction, sexuality, and authority.

In the contemporary period reviewed in this chapter, Pius XI's encyclical letter, *Casti Connubii,* which was issued fifty years after Leo's *Arcanum,* was the first clear articulation of the primacy of procreation as an end. While by no means a new development in Catholic thought, Pius's discussion was significant because it was a response to changing societal attitudes about sex and procreation, especially what appeared to be increasing support for contraception, sterilization, and abortion. Pius XI structures the encyclical around the "three blessings" of marriage: propagation of offspring, conjugal fidelity, and sacramental indissolubility. He derives this threefold description from the traditional Augustinian discussion of marriage.[12] As Elizabeth Clark notes, "The very fact that a head of the Catholic Church in the twentieth century could rest his case so firmly on the teachings of an author who lived a millennium and a half earlier indicates the signal importance of Augustine's writings on marriage and sexuality for the centuries to come" (Clark 1996, 1).

The child is the primary blessing of marriage, according to Pius XI. God uses humans as helpers in the propagation of life. Unlike other creatures, God intends humans to do more than "live and fill the earth." They are born "that they may be worshippers of God." God made humans part of the supernatural order, and that status in turn makes human offspring "a gift of divine goodness." This gift, however, must be returned, as it were. The proper education of children involves "offering" them to the Church so that they will "become members of the Church of Christ . . . fellow-citizens of the Saints, and members of God's household." The offering refers to the sacrament of baptism, which sanctifies the offspring. Pius reiterates the Catholic doctrine of the transmission of original sin through "the very natural process of generating life" (Pius XI 1930, 9).

The propagation and proper education of offspring as a blessing and benefit of marriage has a corresponding evil or vice: actively avoiding procreation either through "frustration of the marriage act," abortion, or sterilization. A large segment of the encyclical deals with the problems surrounding the regulation of births. Many have viewed Pius's discussion of this issue as a response to the Anglican Church's 1930 Lambeth conference that officially lifted its ban on the use of artificial contraception by married couples.[13] Furthermore, debates about the use of sterilization, particularly for eugenic purposes, were rampant in the early part of the twentieth century. The discussion of abortion is interesting because it appears to address only situations where the mother's life is in danger. In other words, it is not framed in the contemporary language of women's choice. Nevertheless, Pius XI deems it illicit regardless of the particular circumstances.

Pius XI articulates the Catholic position that (virtuous) continence is an accepted way to avoid offspring. Any attempt to frustrate the marriage act—in other words, to try to derive sexual pleasure from an act while purposely preventing the conception of offspring—is intrinsically against nature. Thus, no reason, however serious, can justify or make good such an act. The belief that the sexual act is intrinsically disordered when conception is prevented stems from the view that the nuptial union ought to remain chaste. In other words, the sex act is a natural power intended to create life. Any pleasure that humans derive is licit only when they allow the primary purpose (procreation) to occur—when it is a means for achieving the proper end. The message in *Casti* is that couples who are unable to practice continence as a way to avoid conception are wicked and indulgent. The Church, according to Pius, must "stand erect" in the midst of a society that is in moral ruin (a not-so-veiled reference to the Anglican Church decision allowing for artificial methods of contraception).

Pius XI's argument is quite distinct both in substance and structure from post–Vatican II versions of Catholic prohibitions against contraception. Most notable is his concern about pleasure. He echoes the traditional Catholic suspicion of sexual passion and desire, one expressed famously by St. Augustine when he characterized marriage as "a remedy for infirmity and for some a solace for their human nature" (Clark 1996, 82). Augustine also writes, "In marriage, intercourse for the purpose of generation has no fault attached to it, but for the purpose of satisfying concupiscence, provided with a spouse, because of the marriage fidelity, it is a venial sin; adultery or fornication, however, is a mortal sin. And so, continence from all intercourse is certainly better than marital intercourse itself which takes place for the sake of begetting children" (48). A clear hierarchy governs sexual activity, with procreation at the top. While the "satisfaction of concupiscence" might be necessary, Augustine classifies such an act as a venial sin.

Pius XI reaffirms the primacy of procreation in his discussion of sterilization. He comments on two different practices; forced medical sterilization of persons considered unfit to reproduce and state action that prevents persons from marrying if it is felt that they might produce offspring that do not meet the norms of good heredity. Pius XI accepts certain eugenic premises, such as those associated with positive eugenics. He describes attempts to counsel and encourage persons to produce healthier and stronger children as "not contrary to right reason." The discussion of the evils of sterilization reaffirms both the "welfare of the offspring" and "the natural right of man to enter matrimony." One implication of this right is that public authorities cannot prevent persons who are "naturally fit for marriage" from marrying; "the family is more sacred than the state," proclaims Pius XI. Pius XI's condemnation of sterilization focuses on the limits of the state. He argues that "public magistrates have no direct power over the bodies of their subjects." Punishment for a crime, however, is one exception to the limits of state power (1930, 35). Forced sterilization or any other direct harm to the integrity of the body cannot be justified unless a crime has taken place.

Casti Connubii remained the primary official document of Catholic teaching on marriage and procreation until the 1960s, when Paul VI issued *Humanae Vitae*. Nevertheless, most scholars cite Pius XII's 1951 address to the Italian Catholic Association of Midwives as a milestone in the twentieth-century development of marriage doctrine. There, Pius XII reiterates much of the previous official teaching but emphasizes different things. For one, he relies very clearly on the language of the ends of marriage, stating firmly that procreation is the primary end of marriage; all other ends are subordinate. He also emphasizes and develops the language of children as gifts from God, and he undertakes a much more explicit and detailed discussion of contraception, focusing primarily on the issue of "recourse to the periods of natural sterility." It would be imprecise to refer to any of these as genuine innovations in Catholic teaching. Indeed, Pius XII relies heavily on previous church teaching. The differences are less about content and more about tone and scope.

For various reasons, the address to the Italian Catholic Association of Midwives is different in style from the encyclicals issued by Leo and Pius XI. Pius XII is aware of the central role the midwives play in advising couples, especially women, on matters having to do with parenting and sexuality. He even refers to their work as an apostolate and notes that their responsibility to transmit church teaching is a central task.[14] Describing this apostolate to the midwives, Pius XII explains and develops Catholic teachings on issues such as abortion, sterilization, and contraception. While he reiterates the Church's absolute prohibition of all those acts, he contextualizes these prohibitions as part of a larger discussion about procreation as the primary end of sexual intercourse.

He realizes that the midwives' proximity to birth endows them with a strong power to affect and influence Catholic couples, not only on matters pertaining to their professional and technical skills but also on matters of morality. He describes the significant effect they can have in encouraging and reassuring parents about the joys of parenthood, particularly by emphasizing the idea that the child is a gift from God. The extended discussion of children as gifts reinforces the sanctity-of-life theme that is central to the address. It also reinforces procreation as a primary end. One interesting element of the discussion, however, is how differently the father and the mother experience the gift of a child.

For a father, the child is a reward for his righteousness; for the mother, the child enables her to be redeemed. Clearly, for both parents, the task of raising a child is a tremendous responsibility and duty, but the gift of the child functions in different ways theologically. There is an interesting temporal dimension to this gender-based dichotomy. For the man, the child represents a reward for *past* behavior; for the woman, an opportunity for *future* redemption. This pronounced gender difference is certainly not a novelty in Christian thought. It reflects the biological fact that the woman's physical participation in bringing the child into the world is of a different degree than the man's. It seems that the blessings that accrue from the gift result for the woman from the actual act of childbirth. Pius XII states, "God gives the child to the mother, but in giving it, He makes her cooperate effectively in the unfolding of the flower, the seed of which He has sown in her, and this cooperation becomes the way that leads to her eternal salvation: 'Woman will be saved by childbearing' " (Liebard 1978, 106). This emphasis on the importance of maternity is consistent throughout Catholic sexual morality. In the earlier *Casti Connubii,* Pius XI had exclaimed, "and proving herself superior to all the pains and cares and solicitudes of her maternal office with a more just and holy joy than that of the Roman matron, the mother of the Gracchis, she will re-joice in the Lord crowned as it were with the glory of her offspring" (Pius XI 1930, 10).

Pius XII expresses a particular concern in this address to the mid-wives about situations when the child is not seen as gift or blessing but rather as a burden. He urges the midwives "to sustain, to reawaken and stimulate the mother's instinct and the mother's love" (Liebard 1978, 109) in such cases. This requires positive actions of support and encouragement as well as negative actions, namely the refusal to co-operate with any immoral action. Here, he is referring primarily to cooperation in the procurement of abortions or in providing any im-pediments to conception.

In this section, Pius XII reiterates the teachings of his predecessor Pius XI. He states that "any attempt on the part of the husband and the wife to deprive this act of its inherent force or to impede the procreation of a new life, either in the performance of the act itself, or in the course of the development of its natural consequences, is immoral, and furthermore, no alleged 'indication' or need can convert an intrinsically immoral act into a moral and lawful one" (109–110). Pius XII then emphasizes the permanent validity of that precept in order to quell any thoughts that modern understandings of human sexuality might change the normative force of that teaching. One modern view that concerns him in this address is what he refers to as an emphasis on personal values, by which he means attitudes that claim that sex in marriage is primarily an experience of love. He restates the view that the propagation of offspring is the primary end and that while other ends are acceptable, "they are essentially subordinate to it" (116).

Pius XII's address to the midwives is his strongest condemnation of artificial contraception. He focuses, however, on a different prob-lem than his predecessors did, namely on whether "recourse to the periods of natural sterility" as a way to avoid conception is ever licit. The problem with this activity is that the participants clearly intend to avoid parenthood, which he earlier posits as the primary purpose of conjugal sexual activity. Thus, if the couple is seeking sexual plea-sure while intentionally avoiding the birth of a child, it would appear that the primary end or purpose is no longer procreation; it is pleasure for the sake of pleasure. However, he exempts couples who could put forward so-called serious reasons for avoiding pregnancy "on medical, eugenic, economic and social grounds." Thus, "the use of infertile periods can be lawful from a moral point of view" (113). Pius XII's description of serious reasons is general and wide ranging, leaving room for varied interpretations. Nevertheless, he emphasizes that intentionally nonprocreative sex undertaken to satisfy sexual desire is problematic. He warns that if sufficient reasons do not exist and a couple continues "to avoid the fruitfulness of the union, while at the same time continuing fully to satisfy sexual intent," they are exhibiting "a false appreciation of life" and are motivated by immoral standards (113).

The history of Catholic discussions of the ends and purposes of marriage has always included the question of "sterile" couples. It is interesting that, according to John Noonan, much of the discussion in the medieval period concerned the apparent contradiction in church law between allowing "sterile" couples to marry and not allowing "impotent" couples to do the same. "Sterile" couples are physically able to engage in sexual intercourse but are unable to conceive, which raised the problem of nonprocreative sex. "Impotent" couples are not physically able to engage in sexual intercourse, thus are unable to consummate their marriage. Several important values are at stake in this discussion: procreation as the primary purpose of sex, whether seeking pleasure is a legitimate end of sexual acts, and whether all the ends of marriage had to be met to make it valid.

According to Noonan, the practice of permitting the "sterile" to marry was traditionally justified on the basis of Augustine's suggestion that marriage was "the solace of human dignity." Augustine makes this statement in a discussion of whether the sacramental bond of marriage remains indissoluble when procreation is impossible. He argues that Christian marriage is a symbol of stability and therefore cannot be dissolved even if the end of procreation cannot be achieved. Noonan states the theoretical difficulty inherent in this justification in the form of this question, "How could the procreative good be essential to marriage if sterile marriages were valid?" (Noonan 1965, 289). In other words, allowing nonprocreative intercourse undermines the theory of procreative purpose at least to the extent of suggesting that it is not the only legitimate purpose. Bernard Häring explains that marital intercourse of sterile persons was generally condoned on the basis of a desire for a child because it indicated right intention. A couple engaging in intercourse "where there was neither hope nor desire for fecundity" was viewed as showing "a lack of self-control and mortification" (Häring 1993, 154).

The Catholic view of the family, often described in Catholic literature as the domestic Church, reinforces the importance of procreation as justification for sexual intercourse. In the eighteenth and nineteenth centuries, the realm of the home was increasingly perceived as holy and deserving of protection. At the same time that the domestic sphere was being romanticized and idealized by the Church, it was also an important component of the Church's emerging emphasis on social justice. Leo XIII's encyclical *Rerum Novarum,* often considered the founding document of Catholic social thought, discusses the family and stresses its importance as part of a just social order. One can trace this thread through all the important twentieth-century magisterial statements on marriage and family. In *Gaudium et Spes,* for example, we read that "[t]he well-being of the individual person and of human and Christian society is intimately linked with the healthy condition of that community produced by marriage and family" (Abbott 1966, 249). In this construction, the strong family is the foundation of the strong and just society. Catholic teachings on the ethics of sexuality, particularly in the areas of contraception and reproductive technologies, reinforce a certain aspect of that family, particularly the relationship between the structure of sexual acts and their meanings and purposes.

Sexual acts are thus always in service of the family. While the Catholic tradition has consistently considered procreation to be the primary end of marriage, it has stressed not only the act of producing offspring but also the activity of rearing offspring. The family is the locus of that activity and is consequently linked very directly to the morality of sexual activity. This sentiment is summarized in *Gaudium et Spes:* "The family is a kind of school of deeper humanity" (Abbott 1966, 257).

In 1951 and 1958, Pius XII delivered a set of addresses to groups representing the Associations for Large Families of Rome and Italy. These speeches give us a glimpse of the theory of family life that is so profoundly connected to the Catholic theology of marriage. In the 1951 address, Pius XII describes the political, economic, and psychological problems confronting families of that period. His greatest concern, however, was the challenge posed to established "conjugal morals." More specifically, he is worried about any attacks on the sanctity of human life. He proclaims that matrimony is an institution in the service of life. Any actions within that institution that deliberately target human life contradict its basic principle. Pius II's primary focus is abortion, specifically the worry that abortions are sought out by those who do not value and welcome new life into their families. The large families represented by the associations display courage and trust in God by welcoming numerous children into their families. Certain limited ways of "controlling births" can be legitimate and compatible with God's law (Liebard 1978). Here he seems to be referring to the "recourse to sterile periods," or what is popularly referred to as the rhythm method.

These papal addresses articulate the unwavering Catholic view that the family is the central institution of society. They also reveal a growing belief that society had become more suspicious of procreation. In both speeches the pope applauds and encourages large Catholic families who exhibit a "readiness to accept joyfully and gratefully these priceless gifts of God—their children—in whatever number it may please Him to send them" (219). In Pius's view, the large families are a testimony to the Catholic devotion to the sanctity of human life. In the midst of these glowing commendations of large families, however, he acknowledges the difficulties of having a large number of children and supports controlling births in accordance with God's law as a response. He condemns those who question the wisdom of having many children as selfish and unwilling to adhere to God's plan. On a more practical level, Pius XII also claims that large families have always been viewed as a sign and source of physical health.

Large families symbolize the importance of procreation, not simply by providing a justification and meaning for sexual intercourse but also as a sign of God's will, as a way "to offer . . . healthier and larger groups of souls to the sanctifying activity of the holy spirit" (220). According to this view, sexual acts must be open to procreation not only because doing otherwise would frustrate the natural structure of the act but, more positively, because procreation is a duty. Some might question duty as too strong a term; procreation is after all described in the language of gift and of consent. Nevertheless, in these addresses, the emphasis on the larger good that emerges from numerous children suggests a duty that is incumbent on all families.

At the Second Vatican Council, the issue of sexuality within marriage was taken up in the document *Gaudium et Spes*. Many cite the discussion in this document as an important development in Catholic views on the ends of marriage. Moreover, the timing of this document, which was issued in the early 1960s, coincided with the period of intense Catholic debate about contraception. The document avoids the traditional hierarchy of ends, but it does not completely reverse the traditional view. For example, one passage stresses procreation but does not depict it as the primary end: "By their very nature, the institution of matrimony itself and conjugal love are ordained for the procreation and education of children, and find in them their ultimate crown" (Abbot 1966, 250). Another passage addresses the question of ends and their proper ordering more directly: "Hence, while not making the other purposes of matrimony of less account, the true practice of conjugal love, and the whole meaning of the family life which results from it, have this aim: that the couple be ready with stout hearts to cooperate with the love of the Creator and the Savior, who through them will enlarge and enrich His own family day by day" (254).

While the magisterial documents provide evidence of the tensions between the various ends, certain theologians have been much more explicit and direct in airing the precise nature of the difficulties. Many of the developments in the Catholic doctrine of the ends of marriage have been subtle, involving changes of emphasis and language. One instructive example is the discussion of this topic by John C. Ford and Gerald Kelly in 1964.[15] In their survey of Protestant and Catholic personalist views on the ends of marriage, they indicate quite clearly that while there is agreement on the ends, the disagreement surrounds the ranking of those ends. Parenthood and companionship are the labels Ford and Kelly give to the ends, and they describe the way Protestant teaching has changed in the past 100 years to the point that companionships is now perceived as equal to parenthood (which had been primary). Ford and Kelly summarize this new Protestant position by stating that "there is no essential subordination of the ends of marriage to one another. They are at least of equal rank and dignity, and being independent of one another can justifiably be separated" (Ford and Kelly 1964, 13). This separation between the two ends leads to a position that advocates the permissibility of contraception. And this is precisely what Ford and Kelly want to avoid. The authors, speculating about what might be the causes of this Protestant move away from the traditional Christian teaching, cite the growing acceptance by Protestants of "situation ethics," the lack of an infallible teaching authority, the growing belief in modern thought that sexual fulfillment in marriage is a positive value, new discoveries in the realm of biology, and, finally, the "pressures of the population problem" (14).

While it is not surprising that Ford and Kelly would target "lax" Protestant views on this issue, it is interesting that they acknowledge and take seriously contemporaneous Catholic developments, particularly in the area of personalism. They are critical of authors such as Dietrich von Hildebrand, Herbert Doms, and Bernhardin Krempel for going too far in their attempts to develop a personalist philosophy of marriage. Ford and Kelly's project is to forge a middle position between "the exaggerated personalism" of these authors and the "juridical impersonalism" of the Church. In other words, they want to acknowledge the secondary ends of marriage (what they term the personalist ends), but they maintain that these are subordinate to the primary ends. The secondary personalist ends can be justified, in their view, by values articulated in Pius XI's *Casti Connubii:* mutual help, the fostering of mutual love, and the quieting of concupiscence. Ford and Kelly translate these into the terms "life-partnership," "conjugal love," and "sexual fulfillment."

The translation of "quieting of concupiscence" to "sexual fulfillment" captures the profound and serious changes in the modern understanding of the purpose and meaning of human sexuality. The shift from a perception of sexuality as a negative (something to be avoided) to a positive (something to be pursued) is certainly important to note. The early part of the twentieth century was a period of radical writing and theorizing about human sexuality. Presumptions about sexuality that had been in place for most of the history of Western civilization were toppled and replaced by new ideas about both the biology and the psychology of human sexuality. Ford and Kelly's acknowledgment of the "new personalism" can be seen as a sign of the Church's accommodation to these modern views. In fact, the language issued by the Second Vatican Council is firm in its acknowledgement that procreation is not the only purpose of marriage: "Marriage to be sure is not instituted solely for procreation. Rather, its very nature as an unbreakable compact between persons, and the welfare of the children, both demand that the mutual love of the spouses, too, be embodied in a rightly ordered manner, that it grow and ripen." (Abbott 1966, 255).

The shift from procreation as the primary end to more personalist criteria has had a significant impact on Catholic moral theology, especially in its prohibition of artificial contraception. Another consequence, according to Susan Ross, is that challenging "natural law categories of marriage is an implicit challenge to traditional gender roles as they are construed theologically" (Ross 1991, 356). The connection between the description of the ends of marriage and views about gender is an important clue for our study.

CHASTITY

Casti Connubii begins with the line "How great is the dignity of chaste wedlock, Venerable Brethren." The message is clear: married couples ought to strive for chastity in their sexual relations.[16] This logic is based on the belief that chastity (the mastery of the will over passions) is the most effective way to love the other as a person, not as an object. Chaste sexual acts express a more "pure" disinterested love. Conjugal chastity is distinct from continence. It does not require total abstinence from sexual activity—although that can be a legitimate form of conjugal chastity if both parties to the marriage consent to such a relationship. Rather, it describes a certain attitude toward such activity that strives to avoid overvaluing pleasure. The 1994 catechism distinguishes three forms of chastity, each specific to a person's status. Hence, those who profess consecrated virginity express chastity as a complete commitment to God. Those who are engaged to marry practice continence. Married couples express their chastity through appropriate sexual relations with their spouse (United States Catholic Conference 1994, par. 2349). Chastity, in the context of both marriage and celibacy, is based on a "pure love" modeled on the covenant between God and his people as expressed in Christ's love for the Church.[17] Indeed, pure love is defined as the mutual help the couple offers one another for the goal of "forming and perfecting their interior lives." Put differently, marriage is a school for the virtues and the fostering of love for God and for one's neighbors. Chastity, the virtue required for marriage, is ultimately an expression of the virtue of charity.

Consequently, sexual desire and sexual pleasure are not ends in themselves; they are useful means for achieving other ends. The anxiety about pleasure is disguised as fear about selfishness and objectification. According to the pontifical council's 1995 document, "The chaste person is not self-centered, not involved in selfish relationships with other people" (Pontifical Council for the Family 1995, par. 17). While the Catholic tradition has come to acknowledge that sexual pleasure is a legitimate part of sexual relations, the magisterial documents tend to characterize sexual passions as dangerous and difficult to control. The root of this distrust of sexual pleasure can be traced to Stoic influences on early Christian views of the body, expressed primarily as a severe distrust of the body. The New Testament contains numerous references to the dangers of sexual pleasure that, along with Paul's preference for celibacy over marriage, have left a pronounced mark on Christian sexual ethics. Furthermore, several aspects of St. Augustine's theology of marriage and sexuality diminish the role of pleasure. Most prominent, of course, is his insistence that original sin—the sin of turning away from God—has led to the corruption of sexual intercourse. [18] These early Christian attitudes about married sex persist into the contemporary period.[19]

In the period of concern for this study, *Casti Connubii* offers a detailed view of the Catholic attitude to sexual pleasure. As we have seen from the opening sentence of Pius XI's encyclical, he is suspicious of lust and its power in marriage. That is why the proper attitude of spouses toward each other must be grounded in chastity. He writes that "the chief obstacle to this study [the encyclical] is the power of unbridled lust, which indeed is the most potent cause of sinning against the sacred laws of matrimony, and since man cannot hold in check his passions, unless he first subject himself to God, this must be his primary endeavor in accordance with the plan divinely ordained" (Pius XI 1930, 50). In other words, subjection of sexual desires is essentially a religious activity. The proper conjugal relationship is dependent on both parties being "wholly imbued with a profound and genuine sense of duty towards God" (52). Once a person has subjected his or herself to God, with the aid of divine grace, he or she will succeed (even gladly) in controlling his or her passions. The divinely ordained plan is not simply about the physical natural order, it is as much about human limitations, especially the limitations of human reason and will. Pius XI transforms the discussion of subjugation of passions into an entreaty to the faithful to obey the Church. In his view, reason cannot fully perceive the moral laws that regulate marriage. Human sinfulness often clouds that pursuit. Consequently, humans need the Church to guard and teach the truth. Without divine guidance through the Church, humans can never achieve the order inherent in the divinely ordained plan.

Pius XI explains this authority in the context of the need for individual Catholics to be obedient to the Church: "The faithful need to be on their guard against the overrated independence of private judgment and that false autonomy of human reason" (54). He draws an analogy between the role of the Church and revelation; revelation was added to illuminate reason and the Church was constituted to guard and teach the truth. He also addresses a question important to Catholics at that time that has persisted throughout the history of Catholic ethics: If the only licit sex acts are those open to procreation, what of couples that are unable to reproduce? He responds that sexual intercourse in the context of those marriages is not a violation of the natural law. This is because matrimony also has secondary ends "such as mutual aid, the cultivating of mutual love, and the quieting of concupiscence" (30). This acknowledgement that human sexuality has other purposes is important and later documents develop it in more detail.

Pius XI considers conjugal chastity and fidelity to be the second important blessing of marriage, and the greatest threat to them is adultery. The prohibition against adultery is not a new teaching in Christianity; as the encyclical points out, it is founded in the natural law, confirmed by God in the Ten Commandments and by Christ in the Gospels. Fidelity to one's spouse is closely connected to chastity because uncontrolled sexual appetites can lead one to look beyond marriage and perhaps even commit adultery. Pius XI mentions modern attitudes that encourage friendship of either spouse with a third party, or that hold that marriage limits the freedom and action of persons. Corresponding to this vice that would lead some to sanction adultery is the view that "the rights of husband and wife are equal." "False teachers" expound these views by claiming that the attitude of subjection in marriage harms the dignity of persons and therefore ought to be eliminated. Pius XI claims, that these views lead some to call for the emancipation of women. If chastity is an expression of subjugation, both to passions and to authority, then it would appear to be a virtue better suited for women.

This connection between chastity and women's subordination highlights the place of gender in the Catholic view of marriage and family. This emphasis is also present in Leo XIII's earlier encyclical, *Arcanum.* In *Casti Connubii,* this discussion of women's rights occurs in the context of the vice of adultery, not in the context of procreation. A more modern understanding would equate women's rights with their dominion over their bodies. In *Casti,* the connection with adultery is that the call for greater emancipation for women is an expression of a misguided understanding of freedom. A proper understanding of freedom would not view the limits on the options of both men and women in marriage as subjugation. At issue is what Pius XI refers to as a woman's "physiological emancipation," which he defines as freedom "at her own good pleasure from the burdensome duties properly belonging to a wife as companion and mother" (37). He mentions women's social and economic emancipation, but his emphasis on physiology suggests that the disorder of emancipated women is so great that it leads them to desire the wrong things.

Women who seek this sort of equality risk harming not only their husbands and children but also themselves, according to Pius XI. He states, "[F]or if the woman descends from her truly regal throne to which she has been raised within the walls of the home by means of the Gospel, she will soon be reduced to the old state of slavery" (38). The metaphors in this passage are powerful. The throne is a place of high honor, yet it overlooks a limited sphere—"the walls of the home." Pius XI also acknowledges that social and economic conditions might necessitate women's entrance in to the public sphere, and he urges public authorities to enact laws that will protect women, at least in their roles as mothers and wives. The implication is that civic laws are necessary to uphold the "essential order of domestic society" (39).

While the discussion of women's rights appears to be oddly placed in the encyclical since its precise relation to adultery is not clear, the discussion of what constitutes a true bond of marriage seems appropriate. The pope is critical of trends that claim that "a certain vague compatibility of temperament" is more important than a "true, solid love" (39). The problem with the first criterion is that once compatibility disappears, the couple feels that they are no longer in love and turn to other persons or even to divorce.

The Church responds to the vices that threaten marriage by ensuring that the "divinely ordained plan" is restored. The ultimate threat to this plan is "the power of unbridled lust," and the only remedy to these unchecked passions is subjection to God. By being subject to God, humans receive the aid of grace, which enables them to control their own passions. In essence, the pope suggests that without a willingness to be subject to God, humans risk the sin of lust: "the onslaughts of these uncontrolled passions cannot in any way be lessened, unless the spirit first shows a humble compliance of duty and reverence towards its Maker" (52). Consequently, the Church has a duty to make sure that the faithful receive complete instruction about the nature and origin of matrimony in a way that is convincing to their intellect.

The encyclical acknowledges that instruction is not sufficient; married couples must exhibit a steadfastness of will in order to obey the "sacred Laws of God and of nature in regard to marriage" (56). The grace of the sacrament of marriage strengthens the will to obey. So couples must combine obedience to the Church with a strong will to fight off the vices prevalent in society. The emphasis on will in relation to chastity was a central concern of St. Augustine's writing on sex and marriage. He argues that even "the gift" of continence must be willed. He writes, "Who, I say, would have continence if he did not will it?" (Clark 1996, 85). The Church helps by preparing couples for the sacrament, and parents help by imbuing a strong understanding of this sacrament in their children from an early age.

The sacramentality of marriage and the regulation of sexual pleasure are interconnected. The sacramental nature of marriage both assists couples in the practice of chastity and explains to them why they must be chaste. Chastity in essence is a way to display obedience to church teaching and it practice strengthens the will for obedience.

While both the Church and individual couples have an important role to play in maintaining the sanctity of marriage, the state can also intercede in helpful ways. The most interesting example is the role of the state in ensuring that heads of families receive a wage that is sufficient to support a wife and children. In other words, the removal of any external stresses (such as economic ones) from the family strengthens marriages. Here Pius XI echoes an important theme in the Catholic tradition of social teachings.[20] This request for the state to offer positive assistance contrasts to the other passages such as the ones on forced sterilization where the state is explicitly being asked not to interfere.

These early modern documents concerning marriage and sexuality are instructive for several reasons. First, they present in clear terms the issues about marriage that concern the Church. Divorce, adultery, and sterilization (or any impediments to procreation) are the activities most likely to threaten marriage, according to Leo and Pius XI. They emphasize the attributes of marriage by explaining its origin and its part in Christ's redemptive plan. Second, they reveal the ongoing tension between the Church and the world. Third, and in many ways most important for this project, they draw the indisputable connection between the role of women and the strength of the family. Leo XIII and Pius XI emphasize the role of the Church as champion of women's dignity, but they draw sharp limits around the extent to which this dignity translates into freedom and autonomy for women. They articulate a vision of gender complementarity; one that would keep women's roles firmly bound to hearth and home. They imply that the family protects women and ensures that they will fulfill their natural roles as mothers and wives.

John Paul II, writing both as pope and as philosopher (Karol Wojtyla), addresses marriage and sexuality in the context of a very different world than the one Leo XIII, Pius XI, and Pius XII wrote about. He maintains the focus on the doctrine of procreation as the primary end of marriage, but expands the discussions of concupiscence and chastity to include a more generous and positive interpretation of sexual pleasure. In fact, he devotes a large segment of his work *Love and Responsibility* to an analysis of the sexual urge that is based on human experience. Wojtyla makes the claims about human experience on the basis of his pastoral work with married couples. His discussion of sex occurs in the context of what he calls a personalistic norm. In essence, for Wojtyla, personalism is the opposite of utilitarianism. It is a loving attitude toward the other—one that ensures that the other is treated as a person, not merely a useful object. Wojtyla describes the personalistic norm as follows: "[I]n its negative aspect, [it] states that the person is the kind of good which does not admit of use and cannot be treated as an object of use and as such the means to an end. In its positive form the personalistic norm confirms this; the person is a good towards which the only proper and adequate attitude is love" (Wojtyla 1981, 41).

The sexual urge, which he defines as "a natural drive born in all human beings," is not the same as instinct. Instinct is an interior source of specific actions; whereas an urge is an orientation that can be directed and controlled by the human will. Urges are expressed in action, but to reach that expression, a person must take an initiative. By introducing the concept of sexual urge, Wojtyla acknowledges the sexual urge in humans as good, but claims that it must be subordinated to the objective truth that procreation is the primary end of marriage. He describes it another way—the personalistic norm must be synthesized with the natural order. Thus, the sexual urge in humans must always be directed to the ultimate good of conjugal morality—treating the other as a person, not an object to be used.

While John Paul II clearly elevates human sexuality and attends to it more carefully than his predecessors, he retains the basic structure of Catholic sexual ethics. Procreation is the primary end of sex, marriage is a sacrament, and chastity is the primary virtue of marriage. His discussion of chastity, especially in *Love and Responsibility,* is intended to "rehabilitate" this virtue, which he argues that "more than any other, seems to be the virtue which resentment has tended to outlaw from the soul, the will and the heart of man [*sic*]" (144). He attributes this to modern claims that sexual relief is essential to health and that chastity and continence are enemies of love. He claims that his description of integrated love based on a personalistic norm rejects any notion of sexuality that is not ultimately about "the whole-hearted desire of the beloved person's good" (145). Hence, chastity is a means of avoiding making sexual pleasure the ultimate end of conjugal love. If sex is integrated into the entirety of a loving relationship, then it cannot be the element by which the relationship is judged.

The Catholic promotion of celibacy is also undoubtedly connected to the distrust of sexual pleasure that emerges largely from the view that sexual desire is irresistible and uncontrollable.[21] John Paul II offers a different explanation of the link between marriage and celibacy. His primary claim is that marriage and celibacy do not contradict one another; they are mutually confirming. They reinforce and strengthen one another. Renouncing sex "for the sake of the Kingdom of Heaven loses its meaning" if the individual fails to value human sexuality (John Paul II 1981, 16). The sacrifice of sex gains its value from the goodness of sex. Consecrated celibacy serves a different function. It witnesses to the true sacramental meaning of a total gift of self to the Church; in this way, the celibate embodies faith in the Kingdom of God. The self-gift offered in marital sex is thus seen as a mere approximation of the totality of God's gift to humans in the incarnation.

Regardless of the variety of ways that sexual pleasure has been depicted in the tradition, a clear message emerges: the experience of sexual pleasure is justifiable only in the context of procreation. In the Congregation for the Doctrine of Faith's 1975 *Declaration on Certain Questions Concerning Sexual Ethics (Persona Humana)*, the Vatican attempts to describe the virtue of chastity in more positive terms. The authors of the *Declaration* claim that the virtue of chastity is not achieved simply by refraining from certain actions; it also requires the attitude of proper love for the other. As might be expected, they turn to the New Testament writings of St. Paul for the proper construal of chastity. They point out that in addition to the motivations of avoiding harm to one's neighbor or to the social order, there is a "specifically Christian motive" for practicing chastity; namely, that the practice of chastity honors Christ's redeeming action by honoring the body which is the temple of the Holy Spirit" (Congregation for the Doctrine of Faith 1975, XI). The *Declaration,* quoting from Paul's letter to the Corinthians, states, "You are not your own property; you have been bought and paid for. That is why you should use your body for the glory of God" (XI). This passage situates chastity in a theological context by connecting it to both creation and redemption. To sin against one's own body is to sin against God's created order.

The authors of the *Declaration* emphasize another element of the positive, proactive aspect of chastity when they imply that the practice of chastity leads to several positive effects that are not primarily sexual.

First, we are told that chastity has an epistemological effect. By appreciating the necessity of chastity, men and women will be in a position to know sexual moral norms. In the words of the *Declaration,* they will gain "a kind of spiritual instinct" (XI). A second effect that accrues is connected to the first—the ability to understand these norms. Third, they will know "better how to accept and carry [them] out, in a spirit of docility the Church's teaching" (XI). Rather than characterizing chastity merely as an anti-sex stance, the authors emphasize its positive elements. It involves the whole of the moral life; indeed, it sharpens the skills needed for rightly ordered living.

The Pontifical Council for the Family's statement on human sexuality, issued in 1995, is by far the most explicit pronouncement on the important role of chastity. It articulates a view of chastity that extends the centrality of sexuality to personal development: "[S]exuality is not something purely biological, rather it concerns the intimate nucleus of the person" (Pontifical Council for the Family 1995, par. 3). Quoting from the 1994 catechism of the Catholic Church, the statement claims that "[c]hastity means the successful integration of sexuality within the person and thus the inner unity of man in his bodily and spiritual being" (par. 4). This description of chastity reveals the profound influence of personalism on contemporary Catholic views of sexuality. The individual's response to his or her sexuality is seen as definitive for that person's entire being. As the above quote indicates, chastity is about the integration of one's spirit with one's body. The authors of the statement describe the "integration" or "inner unity" in even more psychological terms. They write, "Chastity makes the personality harmonious. It matures it and fills it with inner peace" (par. 17).

The claims about sacrament, procreation, and chastity reflect Catholicism's vision of order and alignment in the theological, political, social, and personal realms. In the next chapter we shall see what happens to this vision of order when it is tested by the debates about regulating reproduction that became especially prominent and public in the 1960s. Preventing pregnancy or achieving it with the assistance of medical interventions challenges the rightly ordered relationship between God as creator and his creation. This view of the theological significance of human procreation is a central component of Catholic magisterial teaching on sexual and reproductive ethics. The sacramental nature of marriage—that which makes it a sign of God's love for humans—affirms the theological order of this human institution. A recurrent theme in these documents is that God—not humans, not the state—regulates marriage and that marriage is the locus of God's creative work.

Similarly, the claim that procreation is the primary end of the sexual act also reflects a concern for order. Like sacramentality, the emphasis on procreation emerges from the rightly ordered relationship of God to humans. However, a different ordered relationship is also implied—one that concerns the realm of the natural. God orders sexual faculties for the end of propagating offspring. Hence, sexual organs must be used only for the purpose for which they were intended. This teleological order, whereby the telos of an object defines its purpose, is based on a belief in the ability of nature to reveal right order. Such a vision of order limits and regulates sexual activity. The emphasis on procreation as the primary end of marriage and as the primary (and sometimes only) justification for sexual intercourse suggests that marriage is also a natural institution. Human sexuality is understood primarily in naturalistic terms, and the moral norms governing sexual behavior rely on the "natural" for justification. Thus, just as the theme of sacramentality emphasizes the vertical dimension of order (God as creator; humans as creatures), procreation emphasizes a horizontal dimension that designates the proper order of the body in relation to the world around it.

The emphasis on chastity draws our attention to order in a different way that is mostly concerned with the internal realm. Self-mastery and self-control are both viewed as prerequisites for the self-giving that characterizes sex in marriage. Thus, even though chastity is an interior stance, it is ultimately other-regarding: "Chastity is the spiritual power which frees love from selfishness and aggression" (Pontifical Council for the Family 1995, par. 16). Chastity, with help from the Holy Spirit, is "the interior order of married life" (par. 21).

Integral to all these senses of order are the views that male and female gender roles are divinely instituted and that the proper ordering of gender roles has normative implications, particularly in the area of sexual morality. The emphasis on sacramentality, especially when focusing on the temporal aspects of sacrament, illustrates this gender theory in a pronounced way. We saw how married couples are believed to reenact the original creation, how they actuate it through their indissoluble bond, and, finally, how marriage allows them to express eschatological hope. The gender implications, primarily in the way that the fatherhood of God is mirrored in man's fatherhood, are significant.

The theme of procreation has perhaps the most significant implications for Catholic attitudes about gender. The Catholic tradition has struggled with St. Augustine's formulation of the threefold ends of marriage and has focused on the ordering of those ends as well as on the necessity of all three to legitimate marriage and sexual activity. While recent years have seen a move away from procreation as the primary end, it still remains central. Gender identities inform the discussion of the purposes and meanings of marriage, since purposes and meanings are derived from the genital structure of the sexual act. Moreover, emphasis on procreation as the primary end implies that maternity is central to women's self-definition. This type of "identification of the human and moral reality with the physical and the biological aspects of the human acts" is an example of what many Catholic moral theologians have referred to as physicalism.[22] As Charles Curran has argued, the implications of physicalism are that "the human being can never interfere with the physical act of sexual intercourse . . . because the physical act of insemination is normative and must always be present" (Curran 1992, 25). Hence, the magisterium has deemed contraception and artificial insemination (even with a husband's sperm) illicit.

In my discussion of chastity, I illustrated the marked parallel between the subjugation of the passions to the will and the subjugation of reason to church authority. An attitude of obedience is necessary to achieve self-mastery and self-control; obedience requires submission to authority. Chastity is not part of the natural order (in the same way that procreation is). It requires supernatural assistance, primarily through grace and through the teaching of the Church. This connection between sexual self-control and obedience to authority can be traced to the Christian tradition's belief that sexual pleasure is dangerous "because it is virtually irresistible" (Gudorf 1994, 82). The view that sexual desire could not be resisted emerged from a belief that sexual pleasure led to a loss of control which made persons irresponsible and caused them to neglect their moral duties (83). The tradition has always viewed engaging in sexual activity purely for the sake of pleasure with suspicion. More recently, especially during the papacy of John Paul II, there has been greater attention to what is gained from sexual pleasure, such as intimacy and enjoyment.

This sacramental theology of marriage is rooted in a metaphorical understanding of God's relationship to humans that relies on spousal and reproductive images. The ordered relationship between man and woman in marriage mirrors the proper order of the believer's relationship to God and to the Church. In this view, the Church is authorized to protect the true meaning of marriage, especially in the activity of reproduction. The rich theological meaning that grounds Catholicism's views about marriage is thus a starting point for understanding how the tradition formulates the moral norms that govern reproductive activities.

REPRODUCTION

3

Marriage and family planning were among the most watched issues at the general meeting of the Second Vatican Council.[1] On October 29, 1964, Cardinal Leo Suenens[2] of Malines-Brussels and Patriarch Maximos IV Saigh of Antioch addressed the general session of the council on these issues. Suenens, directing his remarks to the newly formed Papal Birth Control Commission, challenged the notion that procreation is the only end of marriage: "It may be we have stressed the words of Scripture: 'Increase and multiply' to the point of leaving in the shadow the other divine statement: 'And they will be two in one flesh.' These two truths are central and both are Scriptural. They must clarify each other" (Anderson 1965–1966, 208). Suenens's argument that there was an improper or faulty emphasis on one element of marriage was the basis of his claim that accepting contraception as licit would not be a reversal of Catholic teaching. Rather, as the Church "progresses in the more profound examination of the Gospel, she can and must integrate this Truth into a richer synthesis and reveal the fuller wealth of these same principles" (208). Thus, Suenens could argue that he was not repudiating the truth, simply developing it more fully.

Patriarch Saigh agreed that change was both possible and necessary. He based his reasoning on the pastoral concerns facing a Church whose faithful "are reduced to living outside the law of the Church, far from the sacraments, in constant anguish, unable to find a working solution between two contradictory imperatives, conscience and the normal conjugal life" (209). In addition to his concerns about the practice of Catholics or about the so-called sense of the faithful, Saigh dismissed the traditional view that marriage has a primary and secondary end. He argued that to separate the purposes of marriage is tantamount to severing the integrity of marriage.[3]

By questioning procreation as the primary end of marriage and supporting the view that change in moral teaching on contraception is consistent with the Catholic tradition, the clergymen's speeches revealed one way that order is a central concern for Catholic sexual ethics. In essence, they challenged two existing orders, a teleological order based on a belief in natural law and the order of authority. These two questions about the source of moral order and the power to command obedience to the norms that flow out of the moral order are central to this volume. Pope John XXIII describes authority as "the power to command according to right reason" and, more important, argues that "authority must derive its obligatory force from the moral order" (O'Brien and Shannon 1992, 138). By exploring these challenges as they apply to the Church's contemporary doctrines on contraception and assisted reproduction and the contexts in which these doctrines were formulated, we can deepen our understanding of what happens to the order expressed in the theology of marriage when it is challenged.

In the first part of this chapter I tell the story of the development of Catholic views on contraception and assisted reproduction. It is a story about the official documents and the historical circumstances surrounding them. In the second half of the chapter I look more closely at the moral arguments put forth by these documents and I attempt to show how the desire to maintain order motivates those arguments.

CONTRACEPTION

In 1893, when Leo XIII issued his marriage encyclical, *Aracanum,* he did not mention contraception, sterilization, or any practices related to intentionally nonprocreative sex. He was mostly concerned with church-state relations especially as they affected Christian marriage. Thus, in the first thoroughly modern document on marriage, the Church is silent on the issue that is most identified with Catholic sexual ethics today. Indeed, it is not until the 1930s that the magisterium fully addresses these matters. In the 1930 encyclical letter *Casti Connubii,* Pius XI asserts, "Since, therefore, the conjugal act is destined primarily by nature for the begetting of children, those who in exercising it deliberately frustrate its natural power and purpose sin against nature and commit a deed which is shameful and intrinsically vicious" (1930, 28). Pius XII ratified this statement of church teaching in grave terms in his 1951 "Address to the Midwives." He proclaimed that his predecessor's assertion about contraception was "as valid today as it was yesterday, and it will be the same always, because it does not imply a precept of human law, but is the expression of a law which is natural and divine" (Liebard 1978, 110). The combined effect of Pius XI and Pius XII's prohibitions is straightforward, and this might have been the end of the story, especially if one reads Robert Kaiser's description of the Catholic laity's views about the issue in the late 1950s. Kaiser writes,

> *Few, if any, Catholics challenged that magisterium on birth control. . . . This wasn't something the church could change. Most Catholics (and every bishop) knew that contraception was not wrong because the church condemned it. Rather, the Church condemned it because it was wrong. And an overwhelming majority of Catholics believed that it was so gravely sinful that they could not even be forgiven for it in the confessional (unless they promised to give up this habitual crime against nature). (Kaiser 1985, 5)*

However, as oral contraceptives became increasingly available and after the 1958 ratification of their use by the Anglican Church, the Catholic hierarchy acknowledged the need to review the definitive statements that Popes Pius XI and XII had issued. Leading European theologians of that era, who suggested that the Church could and should change its teaching on this issue and accept the use of the birth control pill in particular, encouraged this perceived need to review church teachings. Pius XII had ruled on the specific issue of the pill in a 1958 address to the Seventh International Hematological Congress in Rome. There he had explicitly condemned its use but allowed for its use in medically indicated cases.[4]

Despite this explicit papal statement on the issue, many theologians in the 1950s and early 1960s continued to question the certitude of the teaching, raising the question of whether use of the pill constituted an action that was different in morally relevant ways from barrier methods of contraception. In the eyes of some, rather than a physical impediment to procreation, it appeared to regulate a natural occurrence (a woman's fertility cycle). An increasing sense that many Catholics were already using various "artificial methods" of contraception further compounded questions about the certitude of church teaching. Nevertheless, the influential American moral theologians Ford and Kelly reiterated in 1964 that the official teachings of Pius XI and Pius XII constituted an unequivocal condemnation of contraceptive acts, including the use of drugs to prevent ovulation, which they characterized as an example of direct sterilization. By the time the Second Vatican Council was convened, the battle lines had been drawn.

Second Vatican Council

The council, with its emphasis on responding to "modern" problems in society, seemed the ideal forum for exploring the Church's teaching on contraception, especially on the matter of the birth-control pill. In the convocation address, Pope John XXIII evoked the sense that the Church needed to bring "the modern world into contact with the vivifying and perennial energies of the gospel." The modern world, he argued, is a "world which exalts itself with its conquests in the technical and scientific fields" (Abbott 1966, 703). The birth-control pill was such a conquest, and while *Gaudium et Spes* (*Pastoral Constitution on the Church in the Modern World*) includes a few paragraphs on the issue and even mentions contraception, Pope John XXIII delegated the full discussion of the issue to the Papal Birth Control Commission.[5]

Nevertheless, *Gaudium et Spes* did challenge the vision of marriage and sex espoused in *Casti Connubii,* especially on the issue of procreation as the primary end of sex. So, for example, while stating that "marriage and conjugal love are by their nature ordained toward the begetting and educating of children," the authors also state that "marriage to be sure is not instituted solely for procreation" (255). This shift of emphasis in the ordering of ends had already begun, albeit in a small way, in *Casti* when Pius XI proclaimed that the purpose of marriage is more than merely the propagation and education of children but could be seen "more widely as the blending of life as a whole and the mutual interchange and sharing thereof" (Pius XI 1930, 14). *Gaudium* takes the subtle shift of emphasis in *Casti* and makes it much more explicit.[6] In statements such as the following, the authors of *Gaudium* downplay the role of procreation as the primary end of marriage: "Marriage persists as a whole manner of communion of life, and maintains its value and indissolubility, even when offspring are lacking," and "marriage to be sure is not instituted solely for procreation" (Abbott 1966, 255).

While there is no conclusive statement about the morality of the birth-control pill in *Gaudium,* the authors offer a strongly worded injunction about the authority of the Church to teach on such matters: "Sons [*sic*] of the Church may not undertake methods of regulating procreation which are found blameworthy by the teaching authority of the Church" (256). One might see this statement as an affirmation of the views of Pius XI and Pius XII on contraception. In other words, *Gaudium* was saying that the Church has taught authoritatively on this issue and the faithful must obey. It was possible, however, to view the postponement of the detailed discussion of the issue, as well as the text's deemphasis of procreation, as evidence that the teaching was open to change. It was this opening in the text that led some Catholics to challenge the order of the Church's teaching authority.

The explicit reference to the concept of "responsible parenthood" provides another piece of evidence that a shift in the understanding of marital sexuality was occurring. The authors of *Gaudium et Spes* acknowledge that while there are other purposes to matrimony, the transmission of life is the central one. Notwithstanding, they encourage parents to "thoughtfully take into account both their own welfare and that of their children, those already born and those which may be foreseen" (Abbott 1966, 50). More specifically, they urge couples to "reckon with both the material and the spiritual conditions of the times as well as their state in life" (254). The decision about when to have children belongs to the parents, who have the responsibility to make it "governed according to a conscience dutifully conformed to the divine law itself" and with an attitude "submissive toward the Church's teaching office, which authentically interprets that law in light of the gospel" (254).

The point the authors want to make is that "sincere intentions" or motivations are not sufficient evidence for determining what constitutes the "responsible transmission of life." So-called objective standards are needed that are "based on the nature of the human person and his [*sic*] acts."[7] These standards must "preserve the full sense of mutual self-giving and human procreation in the context of true love"

(Abbott 1966, 256). Notable in these passages is the presence of personalist language that emphasizes the whole human person rather than just the physical act. Bernard Häring describes this view of conjugal love as "fully human, personal, total. . . . Conjugal love is not regarded one-sidedly as limited to the marital act, but as pervading the whole of life" (Häring 1967, 237). The personalist strain is even stronger in the Papal Birth Control Commission document *Schema for a Document on Responsible Parenthood* written two years later and, as we shall see, both *Humanae Vitae* and *Donum Vitae* rely heavily on the language of the dignity of the person. The emphasis on the dignity of the human person signals the beginning of a complex debate about the precise meaning of the nature and totality of the human person that continues to this day.

Papal Birth Control Commission

The history and development of the Papal Birth Control Commission[8] is interesting for a variety of reasons, not least of all the novel inclusion of laity in church deliberations, but in the end Pope Paul VI chose to reject its recommendations. Some Catholics understood this rejection as an abuse of papal authority and a violation of the spirit of collegiality and democracy affirmed at Vatican II.[9] The final commission report, *Schema for a Document on Responsible Parenthood,* is worth examining in some detail (McClory 1997, 171–187).[10] It reveals some of the important benchmarks in the Catholic debate about controlling reproduction. The majority of the commission members saw the question of the immutability of church doctrine as the primary obstacle to revising the teaching. They also saw the need to understand the doctrine in light of new developments as the most compelling reason for revising the teaching. Put another way, the commission report is framed by the questions Can the teaching change? Should the teaching change? and What would count as change? In the language of our study, then, the commission report challenges the order of the ends of conjugal morality and the order of the magisterial authority of the Church.

The issue of immutability was a difficult one, especially in light of Pius XI's teaching that contraception was an intrinsic evil, which means that it could never be allowed. Moreover, while Pius XII clearly endorses his predecessor's general teaching on the intrinsic evil of contraception, he allows that the regulation of births through recourse to a woman's fertile periods is licit. In his 1951 "Address to the Midwives," he states that "the use of infertile periods can be lawful from the moral point of view and, in the circumstances which have been mentioned [in a previous sentence, he mentions medical, eugenic, economic, and social grounds] it is indeed lawful" (Liebard 1978, 113). This appeared to some on the commission to challenge the description of all contraception as intrinsically evil, since couples using the rhythm method clearly intend sexual pleasure without the goal of procreation. *Gaudium's* emphasis on "responsible parenthood" further reflected the notion that sexual acts could be undertaken without the intention to procreate. This left the commission with the problem of how to find a way to affirm the teaching that procreation is the primary end of marriage while allowing for intentionally nonprocreative sex.

The record of the discussions held during commission meetings is scant, but Robert McClory's book *Turning Point,* based largely on interviews with Patty Crowley, one of the lay members of the commission, reveals the importance of the immutability issue. McClory notes that the issue of whether Catholic doctrines could be reformed pitted theologians against each other. The Spanish Jesuit Marcelino Zalba articulated the anti-reformability position. He claimed that the tradition was infallible on this issue as evidenced by "the practically uninterrupted tradition" on this doctrine. According to McClory, Zalba cited "the centuries-old condemnation of *coitus interruptus,* the teaching of procreation as marriage's primary end, and the prohibition of direct sterilization, all constituting a universal pattern" (McClory 1995, 70). Dissenting from this view were theologians such as Philippe Delhaye and Bernard Häring, who argued that *Casti Connubii* should be regarded as a pastoral document, not an infallible doctrine. Häring reportedly argued that "infallibility and irreformability pertain only to matters of divine revelation . . . and not to interpretations of the natural law" (70).

The final report of the commission responds to all these theologians. It claims that changes and developments in the modern world can be considered, and even accepted, without damaging the immutability of church doctrine. The report characterizes the acceptance of various means of contraception as a deepening of the Catholic doctrine of marriage and its essential values rather than as an abrupt change: "The doctrine on marriage and its essential values remains the same and whole, but it is now applied differently out of a deeper understanding" (179). To support their claim that the Church could evolve without actually departing from its immutable objective truths, they point to the gradual evolution evident in the marriage teachings of Leo XIII, Pius XI, and Pius XII. According to the report, Leo XIII did not give much attention to the topic, Pius XI was explicit but stressed that more than one value was reflected in the conjugal act, and Pius XII allowed for the use of the rhythm method, which essentially sanctioned human interference in the regulation of births.

The commission report makes the following claims about contraception: First, the regulation of conception is in itself a necessity and a good for modern couples. Second, "decent and human means for the regulation of conception" are necessary (176–177). Third, human intervention in natural processes, when directed to the "essential values of marriage," is objectively good (177). Fourth, the value of marriage cannot be judged on the basis "of the direct fecundity of each and every particular act" but rather that the acts take meaning from their ordering in "a fruitful married life"—"one which is practiced with responsible, generous and prudent parenthood" (177).

The report also evaluates the moral acceptability of intervention in physiological or natural processes. The concern about such interventions is pertinent in light of the argument against contraception as a sin against nature that Pius XI put forth in *Casti*. He states that "[s]ince therefore, the conjugal act is *destined primarily by nature* for the begetting of children, those who in exercising it deliberately *frustrate its natural power and purpose sin against nature* and commit a deed which is shameful and intrinsically vicious" (Pius XI 1930, 28; emphasis mine). The commission report argues that such interventions reflect human sharing in God's creative work and that furthermore it is the cultural mission of the human to "use what is given in physical nature in a way that he [*sic*] may develop it to its full significance with a view to the good of the whole person" (McClory 1995, 177).

The role of natural law in the moral justification for prohibiting contraception differs quite significantly in these two documents. In *Casti,* violating or impeding natural ends is sinful; in the commission report, "the good of the whole person" replaces nature as the ultimate end of moral action. The commission's emphasis on the good of the person echoes the personalism of many of the Second Vatican Council documents and reveals a particular interpretation of the principle of totality that views the whole as more than the physical body. These two different models of natural law can be compared using visual metaphors. Pius XI's vision in *Casti* suggests a linear view of the natural world whereby all physical phenomena tend to a given end and moral norms can and ought to be derived from this physical reality. The commission, by invoking the principle of totality, relies on a more spherical image, one that argues that the sexual activity of the body can only be evaluated morally when it is understood in the context of a larger whole that extends beyond the physical body. These two interpretations suggest two very different models of moral order.

The final theological obstacle the commission report notes is the matter of the intrinsic evil of contraception. It is interesting that the authors avoid using the term "intrinsically evil," but it is clear from the nature of their moral argument that they reject its validity. To say that an act is intrinsically evil is to say that no concrete situation, intention, or potential consequence can justify that act. According to this view, performing a sexual act while intentionally impeding its procreative potential is always evil, even in the case of an extreme, life-threatening situation. The authors of the commission report present a vastly different position. The definition of responsible parenthood as "generous and prudent" is an early hint of their difference in outlook. Prudence is defined in Catholic moral theology as "the virtue that disposes practical reason to discern our true good in every circumstance and to choose the right means of achieving it" (United States Catholic Conference 1994, 1806). The use of the term "prudent" suggests that the married couple will apply their practical reason to the particular circumstance, and that is exactly what the commission report recommends, emphasizing the point that couples must apply objective criteria concretely with a rightly formed conscience. Clearly the use of the term "objective" is intended to deflect any accusations of subjectivity in the method that the report advances. One could argue about whether the use of the term "objective" successfully removes the aura of subjectivity, especially when one considers the list of objective criteria the document offers—items such as considerations of effectiveness and economic situations.

However, the passage that commends carrying out actions that would produce the least amount of physical evil is the most controversial. Physical evil is a moral concept that is meant to stress the distinction between moral evil (evil that comes about as the result of direct intention) and general evil that exists in the world and is not the direct result of human action.[11] The authors of the report also use the term "negative element" to convey the meaning of physical evil. They argue that every method of contraception carries with it some of this negative element. The objective criterion requires that couples choose the means that "carries with it the least possible negative element, according to the concrete situation of the couples" (McClory 1995, 182). This notion of weighing negative elements and choosing the least negative one appears to employ a "utilitarian calculus"—an accusation that is anathema in Catholic moral theology.[12] Closely related to this approach is situation ethics, which Catholicism has rejected roundly. The commission report's utilitarian and situationist leanings conflict with the Vatican's teaching on intrinsically evil acts.

"I don't think there was a doubt in any of our minds that the Pope would follow the Commission report," said Patty Crowley, "after the endorsement of all those theologians and the cardinals and bishops" (128). So it appeared to many of the commission members, but two years later, when Paul VI issued his encyclical on contraception, the endorsement of the majority mattered little. In the period between the completion of the commission's work and the issuance of *Humanae Vitae* (1966–1968), many Catholics felt that the Church's position on contraception was in a state of uncertainty. Papal statements that the issue needed further intense study, the publication of the Papal Birth Control Commission report (it was apparently leaked to the press), and statements by theologians suggesting that Catholics were not bound to obey a doubtful law undoubtedly bolstered this perception (132–133). The urgent need for a papal pronouncement mounted with each passing month.

Humanae Vitae

The encyclical letter that was finally issued on July 25th, 1968, firmly rejected many of the conclusions and much of the reasoning of the commission's report. Monsignor Ferdinando Lambruschini, who introduced the encyclical at a press conference, apparently "noted twice that the encyclical did not represent infallible teaching." However, as an authentic pronouncement of the magisterium, it requires "loyal and full assent, both interior and exterior." He concluded by stating that those who believe otherwise "must change their views and give the example by full adhesion" to the encyclical's teaching (McClory 1995, 138).[13] That Lambruschini mentioned the matter of assent to the magisterium shows the concern about the implications of *Humanae Vitae's* issuance. Debates about questions of dissent, individual conscience, natural law, and papal authority—all matters that were pushed to the forefront by the encyclical—have received much attention in Catholic moral theology in the intervening decades.[14] To begin with, the encyclical unequivocally affirms the authority and competency of the magisterium to rule on this issue. Pope Paul VI's affirmation is uttered as part of his response to the work of the commission. He thanks the commission members for their hard work, but explains that he was compelled to reject their findings because their proposed solutions "departed from the moral teaching on marriage proposed with constant firmness by the teaching authority of the Church" (Paul VI 1968, par. 6).

As a papal encyclical, *Humanae Vitae* is brief and direct. Its argument is constructed around several key points. The letter begins with a summation of the contemporary problems that have given rise to questions about whether the traditional norm that prohibits artificial contraception is open to revision. Central to this summary is an acknowledgment both of the reasons that some theologians have presented in favor of a change in teaching, and new conditions in society that might require a change in teaching. In particular, Pope Paul VI cites rapid demographic developments, the changing place of women in society, the increased value attributed to conjugal love in marriage, and progress in the domination and rational organization of the forces of nature by humans (par. 2). All of these have led to questions about revising ethical norms and making them more appropriate for today's conditions.

In addition to evolving societal views and circumstances, the pope acknowledges another argument in favor of revising the teaching on contraception. He claims that some have suggested that the "principle of totality" offers a sufficient foundation for justifying artificial contraception. Some theologians perceive the principle as an affirmation of the complex relation of whole to parts. Pope Pius XI had relied on the principle to support his prohibition of sterilization in 1930. This principle continues to be a central feature of Catholic bioethics, but as Pope Paul VI notes in *Humanae,* some have suggested that its "field of application" be extended to include contraception. He describes two ways that this principle might be used to defend contraception. First, it could imply that a good intention can transform the nature of an act. Thus, responsible parenthood might be seen as a sufficiently good intention to transform the act of contraception from something evil to something good. Second, it could support the view that the goal of procreation is best judged in terms of "the ensemble of conjugal acts" rather than the single isolated act. In both these instances, the principle of totality means that the whole transcends the individual parts. The problem rests with how to identify the whole. Is it the body? Is it the marital relationship? Or is it the greatest good of the family? Pope Paul also acknowledges the affiliated claim that prohibiting humans from regulating births forces them to succumb to biological rhythms.

He rejects this line of reasoning and in part two of the letter articulates the principles that support the prohibition against artificial reproduction. He draws these principles from a concept that is basic to Catholic moral teaching—the natural law and its connection to God's design. Paul VI argues that conjugal love is not the effect of chance or natural forces; it is part of God's design and, more precisely, part of his objective moral order. The design has a clear normative content and structure. Thus, the twofold inseparable purpose of uniting the couple and transmitting life makes the sexual act in marriage noble and worthy. As humans we can be certain about this design and its normative implications because of our capacity to know the natural law, which, according to the encyclical, is "inscribed in the very being of man and woman" (Paul VI 1968, par. 12). More precisely, the capacity to generate new life is inscribed in the very being of the person. As a consequence, the pope views any contraceptive as destroying part of the meaning and purpose of marital sexuality. He writes that people of the day are "particularly capable of seizing the deeply reasonable and human character of this fundamental principle" (par. 12).

Thus, any act that intentionally renders procreation impossible deprives sexuality of its meaning—of that which makes it noble and worthy. Pope Paul VI repeats a central tenet of Catholic moral theology—no consequence or circumstance can make an intrinsically disordered act good. The encyclical punctuates this quintessentially deontological argument by rejecting both the recourse to the "lesser of two evils" arguments and the "ensemble of the conjugal life" argument.

In the previous chapter, we mentioned the problem that marital intercourse raises for couples known to be sterile. We noted that in general, if the couple desired and hoped for fecundity, their sexual act was considered morally legitimate. *Humanae Vitae* offers a slightly different justification for this case. The encyclical claims that such acts "do not cease to be lawful if, for causes independent of the will of husband and wife, they are foreseen to be infecund, since *they always remain ordained towards expressing and consolidating their union*. In fact, as experience bears witness, not every conjugal act is followed by new life. God has wisely disposed natural law and rhythms which, of themselves, cause a separation in the succession of births" (par. 11; emphasis mine).

The apparent distinction between natural and artificial means of contraception is a serious point of contention in the Catholic teaching on contraception. The distinction seems to imply that Catholic moral theology opposes interventions just because they are unnatural, and that is simply not true. The issue at stake is not an absolute protection of the natural from human intervention but rather whether those interventions represent a misuse of the natural or a disordering of the natural course of events. So engaging in marital sexuality is natural and good, but doing so while obstructing that particular act from achieving its natural telos is an abuse. Put differently, it is a matter of a proper ordering of the relationship of humans to "the natural," which is another way of saying the participation of humans in God's design. Thus, while the intention of a couple who uses the rhythm method of birth control is the same as that of a couple who uses the birth-control pill, the effect of their action on the natural telos of a particular act is different. In one case, the couple "controls" nature by using its natural rhythms. In the other case, the couple "interferes" with the natural structure of the sexual act. This view bases the proper understanding of human dominion over nature on the distinction between use and manipulation. The encyclical captures this distinction using the following language: the rhythm method "makes legitimate use of a natural disposition," while artificial contraception "impedes the development of a natural process" (par. 16). What distinguishes these two acts further, according to the pope, is that even though in both cases the will intends the same thing ("avoiding children for plausible reasons"), the rhythm method asks the couple to abstain from sex, which is seen as "proof of a truly and integrally honest love"(par. 16).

It is interesting to note how this particular appeal to nature in support of a moral position differs from that of Pope Pius XI in *Casti Connubii*. There, Pius XI had argued that contraceptive acts deliberately frustrate the natural purposes of human sexuality. He understood sex as destined by nature for procreation; its natural power tends to a very specific end—the generation of life. By contrast, *Humanae Vitae* refers not only to the purposes of acts, but also to their meanings. It describes "the natural structure" of sex as being inscribed not just in the bodies of men and women but also in their very beings. The natural purpose of sex is part of God's design; more precisely, it is a gift from God. The difference between Pius XI and Paul VI's discussion of the natural purposes of sex is not overwhelming, but Paul VI's language evokes a more intimate relation between the act, the person, and God. The 1987 magisterial document *Donum Vitae,* which I discuss later in this chapter, uses the imagery of gift and "the nature of the human person" to even greater effect.

Pope John Paul II has reiterated *Humanae Vitae*'s clear and definitive teaching on contraception in various forms, most notably in his encyclical letters *Evangelium Vitae* and *Veritatis Splendor* and his apostolic exhortation *Familiaris Consortio.* He continues to affirm, at least from the perspective of the magisterium, the authority of the teaching. Immediately after the issuance of *Humanae Vitae,* Catholic moral theologians engaged in intense debate about the authority of the document. Most significant was a statement issued by Catholic theologians in the days following the encyclical's publication. In the statement, they claim that while they "respectfully acknowledge a distinct role of the hierarchical magisterium (teaching authority) in the Church of Christ," they also affirm the special responsibility of theologians to evaluate and interpret the magisterium's pronouncement" (Curran and McCormick 1993, 135).

While they state their clear support for most of the encyclical, they take exception with two aspects: the implied ecclesiology and the methodology used in the document. By ecclesiology, the theologians are referring to what they perceive as a narrow view of what the concept "Church" entails. They accuse the encyclical of equating "Church" with "hierarchical office" and of expressing a "narrow and positivistic notion of papal authority" (136). In other words, the encyclical does not give due attention to the notion of collegiality in the Church. In essence, they claim that these two aspects contradict the "Church's self-awareness as expressed in and suggested by the acts of the Second Vatican Council" (135). Their concern with methodology rests on concerns about the natural law basis of the argument. They claim that the encyclical is "based on an inadequate concept of natural law," one that ignores the multiple forms of natural law; this is simply another way of criticizing the derivation of moral norms from the physical/biological structure of acts—what we earlier identified as physicalism.

The statement of dissent by the Catholic theologians is merely one element in an array of heated arguments that were not limited to those of theologians. In fact, the most serious dissent came from bishops throughout the world,[15] and many lay Catholics interpreted the issuance of *Humanae Vitae* as a betrayal of the promise of Vatican II. The public statements by these theologians and bishops as well as the more private reflections of lay Catholics emphasize the point that Pope Paul VI's encyclical letter on the regulation of birth was just as much about change, authority, and methodology as it was about contraception. Joseph Selling refers to the "Humanae Vitae event" to capture the sense that it was not only the promulgation of the letter but also its acceptance that "raised questions about the exercise of authority in the Church, both teaching authority and disciplinary authority" (Selling 1998, 22).

ASSISTED REPRODUCTION

In contrast, the history of the ethics of Catholic teaching on reproductive technologies, especially the earlier focus on issues such as artificial insemination and in vitro fertilization, has been much less fraught. In fact, it has often been overshadowed by the lively history of the developments surrounding the Catholic doctrine of contraception. More recently, there has been more attention to the protracted debates on abortion, stem-cell research, and cloning. The history of church doctrines on assisted reproduction have also been less dramatic because of the rapid pace of this technology's development and availability to the public, the variety of practices the category "reproductive technologies" encompasses, and the limited relevance of these technologies to Catholic couples.[16]

Early Papal Views on Reproductive Technology

The earliest significant magisterial statement on assisted reproductive technology (ART) appears in a speech Pope Pius XII gave to the 4th International Convention of Catholic Physicians in September of 1949. In the speech, he describes the moral problems associated with artificial insemination and, using concepts central to Catholic moral theology, rules the technique illicit. He quickly condemns artificial insemination outside of marriage or with "the active element of a third person" because of the act's effect on the sacramental indissolubility of marriage. The case of artificial insemination within marriage requires a different response, mostly because he acknowledges that the goal of procreation is a legitimate one for married couples. Nevertheless, he concludes that "[t]hough new methods cannot be excluded a priori simply because they are new, in the case of artificial insemination one should not only keep a very cautious reserve, but must exclude it altogether" (Liebard 1978, 100). He invokes the dignity of the spouses, the well-being of the child, God's creative powers, and the natural law that governs physical acts to support this position. He also reiterates the claim that the means can never justify the end.

Pius XII continued to address these matters in an ad hoc fashion during the next decade of his papacy, primarily in addresses to various Catholic medical associations. One notable occasion was a 1956 address to the Second World Congress on Fertility and Sterility. In that speech, in addition to artificial insemination, he comments on the developing technology of in vitro fertilization, highlighting the tension between the potential benefits and dangers of this technology. Pius XII encourages scientific development, but maintains a cautious tone about its future. He achieves this balance by drawing a line between the technical/scientific significance of the research in "new methods of diagnosis and treatment of sterility in man and woman" and the moral implications of such research. He concurs with the congress's belief that "involuntary conjugal sterility raises an economic and social problem of great significance" (Liebard 1978, 174). The pope is concerned about sterility and wants to encourage the overall scientific project aimed at resolving it. This concern is consistent with the Catholic stress on procreation, but, as we shall see, Catholic responses to reproductive technology have had to find a way to maintain a positive stress on procreation while protecting what Catholics perceive to be the physical integrity of the sex act and procreation. Pius XII writes, "[T]he matrimonial contract does not give this right [to a child], because it has for its object not the "child" but the "natural acts which are capable of engendering a new life and are destined to this end" (178).

Pius XII also expresses sensitivity about the desires of couples experiencing infertility. He reiterates both the spiritual and emotional importance of procreation in marriage. In other words, he does not intend his rejection of assisted reproduction as a diminishment of the Catholic commitment to procreation as the primary goal of marriage. But he indicates that there is a limit to attempts to achieve that goal. That limit concerns what he describes as "the opposite attitude, which could pretend to separate, in generation, the biological activity in the personal relation of the married couple" (176). The pope reminds infertile couples that "the superior fecundity of lives entirely consecrated to God and to neighbor" is an option for them (178). This notion of spiritual fecundity makes sense within the Catholic logic of the superiority of chastity and virginity (especially as it had been articulated up to that historical moment). The goal of increasing the birth rate is a good to be pursued; it is not, however, the ultimate good.

This set of themes and concerns, which mainly revolve around natural law, remained constant throughout the twentieth-century pronouncements on ARTs.[17] It is notable that concerns about the status of the embryo did not become central in magisterial documents until the 1980s, when the Vatican issued documents that offered more fully developed positions on the entire range of available technologies.[18]

Donum Vitae

Donum Vitae, the instruction issued by the Vatican's Congregation for the Doctrine of Faith in 1987, articulates the Catholic opposition to assisted reproduction in detail. Headed by Cardinal Joseph Ratzinger, the Congregation's duty is to promote and protect Catholic doctrine on faith and morals. The instruction explicitly addresses most of the reproductive technologies that were emerging in the late 1980s: therapeutic and nontherapeutic genetic interventions, heterologous (donor gametes) and homologous (spousal gametes) artificial insemination, heterologous and homologous in vitro fertilization and embryo transfer, and surrogate motherhood. It opposes these reproductive interventions, with the exceptions of prenatal genetic testing and therapeutic genetic interventions.[19] These views have remained consistent in the intervening years. John Paul II's encyclical letter *Evangelium Vitae* reiterates the prohibition against these forms of assisted reproduction. More recently, the debates about the morality of stem cell research and cloning have pressed the pope to reaffirm his opposition to the creation of embryos in vitro.[20]

The arguments in the instruction are varied, but three claims emerge as significant: 1) marital sexuality has both a moral and sacred dimension; 2) certain discrete acts, by their inherent structure, can be judged to be objectively evil; and 3) the embryo is a person. These are applied in different ways and with different levels of intensity to evaluations of the various technologies addressed in the document. They share a solid grounding in natural law reasoning. According to the instruction, the fundamental criteria of the moral law are based on the anthropological claim that "the true nature of the person" is corporal and spiritual—a union of body and soul. This "unified totality" of the human person reveals normative truths. In the words of the instruction, the natural moral law "expresses and lays down" norms for conduct that represent more than just biological processes (Congregation for the Doctrine of Faith 1987, Intro. 3); they are the human response to the Creator's call. In short, the Catholic opposition to reproductive technologies stems from a view of moral law as derived from natural law understood as emerging from the "true nature of the person."

The natural law frameworks of *Humanae Vitae* and even the much earlier *Casti Connubii* are visible in *Donum Vitae*. What is different in *Donum Vitae* is the emphasis on a natural law perspective that is connected to the nature of the person. In *Casti*'s brief condemnation of contraception, the appeal to nature had been grounded in a vision of the person's biology, not of the person as a "unified totality." Sex is destined by nature for the begetting of children; it has a natural power to generate life. Thus, anyone who deliberately frustrates its natural power while engaging in sex sins against nature. In *Casti Connubii*'s clear teleological vision, sex has a goal, procreation, and impeding that goal while performing the act is immoral. *Humanae Vitae* does not contradict this message about the natural purposes of sexual acts, but it expands the notion of purpose to include meaning. The language of purposes and meanings moves the argument away from an overly biological understanding of the sex act. The suggestion is that not only do bodies and acts have purposes, but humans have purposes as well. Furthermore, this approach places the natural purpose within the larger context of God's design. While this is implied in *Casti*, Pope Paul VI uses the language of God's design and God's gift more explicitly in *Humanae Vitae*.

In *Donum Vitae*, the metaphor of the gift of life reinforces the importance of personal responsibility. The instruction's foundation is a view of the person as fully integrated—a blend of the bodily and the spiritual. Yet it is in "the body and through the body one touches the person himself [*sic*] as concrete reality" (Intro. 3). The bodily dimension is not, according to *Donum Vitae*, the sole basis of moral norms. The natural law is a "rational order whereby man [*sic*] is called by the Creator to direct and regulate his [*sic*] life and actions and in particular make use of his [*sic*] body" (Intro. 3). Human bodies and human actions fall under the purview of humans, and, according to *Donum Vitae*, moral evaluations are to be made in reference to the dignity of the person.[21] This dignity is best respected when one safeguards the body. The natural law basis of the prohibitions against contraception and assisted reproduction is present in most of the teachings explored for this project. However, there is a pronounced development; the person as a "unified totality" receives an apparently greater status in the moral argument. The language of integrity and totality protects the magisterium from accusations made by some theologians that natural law is wrongly interpreted as too physical or biological. The dignity of the person in *Donum Vitae*'s vision derives from both the body and the spirit of the person.

The early sections of the instruction focuses on the moral status of the embryo. Harming embryos at any stage of their development and for whatever reason is wrong because it violates the respect and dignity they deserve. This view emerges from the anthropological foundation that stresses the union of body and soul. The instruction reaffirms the Church's teaching that "from the first moment of its existence . . . from the moment the zygote has formed" a human individual exists in both her physical and spiritual totality (I.1). This total being exists as the result of God's creative action and reflects the image of its creator. Since the embryo's status as a creature of God ensures its dignity, it is entitled to the same respect given any human being. Any harmful or destructive action that is willfully directed against the embryo usurps the power of God, who is the "Lord of life" (I.5).[22] The issue of harm to embryos is most relevant in discussions of in vitro fertilization, where the standard procedure is to create embryos in a laboratory by fertilizing an egg with a sperm and then placing some of the embryos in the woman's womb. The remaining embryos are usually destroyed, frozen, or donated for research or implantation in another woman's womb. The magisterium perceives all these acts as harms to the embryo.

Concern about harm to the embryo is not the only element of the Church's opposition to these technologies. Even if a technique were guaranteed not to cause harm to any embryos, other moral concerns would make the action illicit. These other moral concerns are part of what Lisa Cahill has termed the "triad of sex, love and procreation" (Cahill 1992, 71). Of course, that triad gains its significance by being properly oriented to God. The instruction claims that "the procreation of a new person, whereby the man and the woman collaborate with the power of the Creator, must be the fruit and sign of mutual self-giving of the spouses, of their love and fidelity" (Congregation for the Doctrine of Faith 1987, II.A.1). Procreative sexual activity must enact the proper relationship of the spouses to God and each other. To disrupt the proper ordering of that relationship by including physicians and technicians is morally troublesome. "The spouses, as parents, co-operate with God the Creator in conceiving and giving birth to a new human being. . . . *God himself is present in human fatherhood and motherhood,*" wrote John Paul II in a later document (John Paul II 1995, par. 43). The list of legitimate participants in the procreative act is clearly delineated. Generating new life in a way that ignores that order usurps God's power. The act of human reproduction has a significant sacral dimension; human intervention in reproduction runs the risk of impinging on that cosmic order.

Donum Vitae also addresses human interventions through the metaphor of human dominion over nature. Quoting Pope John Paul II, the authors express their suspicion of technologies that can lead humans "to the temptation to go beyond the limits of a reasonable dominion over nature" (Congregation for the Doctrine of Faith 1987, I.1). They describe the limits of this dominion in terms of the human ability to ascribe meaning and purpose that is essentially moral to these technologies. These technologies derive their morality less from their intrinsic value and more from their position in relation to human dignity—the sign of God's creative love.

This theological framework grounds the notion that human fertilization must be the fruit of a specific sex act that occurs in the context of marriage. The claim is also supported by an appeal to the potential child's dignity. For example, a child who comes about as a result of in vitro fertilization is deprived of her "proper perfection" because she is conceived outside of a marital sexual act. In other words, the child's full dignity is respected only in the context of a sexual act between married persons, an act that makes the couple "cooperators with God."[23] This argument is connected to the idea that each sexual act in marriage has cosmic significance. The husband and wife, in giving their bodies to one another, are enacting both the gift that God gives them and the potential gift of the child. In this context, dominion over nature is "reasonable" only to the extent that the act of procreation is sexual and confined to the spouses and God. Couples that use these technologies transgress the reasonable limits of procreative activity. Inviting doctors and biologists to participate in procreation risks even-more-serious transgressions. While science and medicine can offer helpful therapeutic resources, they expose humans "to the temptation to go beyond the limits of reasonable dominion over nature" (Intro. 1).

Heterologous artificial insemination, surrogate motherhood, and in vitro fertilization that involves an extramarital donor all violate the main criterion of "a truly responsible procreation," that the child be the fruit of marriage. Marriage is "the only setting worthy of truly responsible procreation" (II.A.2). According to the instruction, such procedures violate the child's "filial relationship with his parental origins" (II.A.2). The child is entitled to be born and raised in a family with the security of knowing that he or she is genetically connected to his or her parents. These procedures also violate the objective structure of the conjugal act and interfere with the "reciprocal self-giving" which is central to marriage and sexuality. In addition to the harm caused to child and to family, the instruction warns against the potential consequences for society at large: "[W]hat threatens the unity and stability of the family is a source of dissension, disorder and injustice in the whole of social life" (II.A.1). In this argument, the authors invoke the inseparability of ends, the belief that the judgment of moral acts must be based on their objective structure, and the potential consequences to society.

The appearance of *Donum Vitae* elicited relatively little controversy, especially in contrast to the response to *Humanae Vitae* two decades earlier. The one prohibition that puzzled many Catholics was the prohibition against artificial insemination using the spouse's gametes (homologous artificial insemination).[24] While they understood concerns about donor sperm or about harm that might befall the embryo during in vitro fertilization procedures, the procedure of artificial insemination by spouse seemed different, since it appeared that the child would be the "fruit of marriage." The primary response by the magisterium to this point was to appeal to the inseparability of the two meanings of the conjugal act. When this type of technology is a "substitute for the conjugal act," it is described as a "voluntarily achieved dissociation of the two meanings of the conjugal act." In other words, intending the end of procreation is not sufficient to justify the use of these technologies. Without the sexual relationship "called for by the moral order," the act is "deprived of its unitive meaning" (II.B.6). It is interesting that these critiques echo the sorts of concerns connected to contraception—concerns about the structure of the act as the ultimate locus for justifying moral behavior. While in the aftermath of *Humanae Vitae,* criticism was focused both on matters of authority and methodology, the responses to *Donum Vitae* appear to have been limited to questions about methodology.[25]

REPRODUCTION AND ORDER

Within the Catholic tradition, as with most of Christianity, sexual activity is governed by a concern for order. For instance, marriage is the only relationship where sex is justified, and even within marriage, both the purpose of sex and the precise nature of the act are severely limited. As we have seen in our survey of twentieth-century Catholic views on marriage, sex, and reproduction, procreation is perceived as the most important end of sexual intercourse; sex is justified when it is ordered to that end. This teleology of sex is supported by appeals to scripture, the view that sexual organs have specific purposes, a sacramental understanding of marriage as mirroring the covenant of God with his people, and an acceptance of the Augustinian tradition's view of the three ends of marriage, *proles* (children), *fides* (fidelity), and *sacramentum* (the sacramental bond).

Having established procreation as a necessary (albeit not a sufficient) justification for sex, we might safely conclude that intentionally nonprocreative sex is suspect. Indeed, Catholic teaching argues that intentionally undermining or impeding the procreative end of a sexual act is intrinsically evil. It is licit, however, for a couple to intend avoiding conception by limiting sex to the nonfertile period of a woman's cycle. Similarly, couples that are knowingly infertile can licitly engage in sexual activity. So, in essence, it is not simply an issue of whether the couple intends procreation or not. Rather, it is a matter of whether a couple engages in a sexual act while at the same time engaging in another act—the act of intentionally impeding procreation by using an anti-ovulant or a barrier method of birth control. The moral problem occurs when the two acts (intentionally nonprocreative sex and intentional impediment to procreation) are undertaken simultaneously, when the couple intends to avoid a pregnancy *and* they actively do something to achieve that end. What is clear in this logic is that intention alone does not justify the act. Certain acts, according to Catholic moral theology, are evil by their very object, regardless of intention or circumstance.

If procreation is a primary good and intentionally nonprocreative acts are illicit, it might seem that all intentionally procreative acts are good and acceptable. Catholic teaching rejects that view. The main instances of problematic intentionally procreative acts are sex outside of marriage and assisted reproductive technologies. To intend procreative sex outside marriage violates the sanctity of marriage as well as the prohibition against extramarital sex. Acts of assisted reproductive technology are a different species altogether, mainly because they are not usually sexual (in the sense that sexual intercourse between man and woman is not required). Thus, rather than a failure to meet the rule of procreation, these acts fail to serve as a proper mode for the transmission of life because they deprive procreation of its complete meaning. These two types of acts—intentionally nonprocreative sex acts combined with acts that intentionally impede procreation or procreative acts that are nonsexual—are absolutely prohibited by the Catholic Church. In both cases, the prohibition stems from a perception that the "complete meaning" of sexual acts entails two necessary and fundamentally inseparable components: procreative potential and sexual intercourse. This perception about complete meaning is embedded in a nexus of claims and beliefs about marriage, family, sex, and nature.

In this section, I explore the justification and defense of Catholic moral teachings about these two types of prohibited acts—artificial contraception and assisted reproduction.[26] These teachings, while distinct, intersect and overlap both in content and history. Furthermore, they both reflect the Catholic concern for order and regulation in the three areas outlined in the previous chapter: 1) the order of the supernatural to the natural as exemplified by the sacramental aspect of marriage, what I call the vertical dimension of order; 2) the ordering of body parts to functions and of sexual characteristics to gender identities—a view that is reinforced by the emphasis on procreation as the primary end of sex, what I call the horizontal dimension; and 3) the ordering of the passions to the will through the practice of the virtue of chastity, the interior dimension of order. Each component of the prohibitions against contraception and ARTs mirrors one of these three types of order. So, for example, the magisterium understands interference with procreation to be interference with God's design—the supernatural dimension informs the morality of natural behavior. In the realm of the natural, body parts have a given telos that limits their acceptable moral uses. The emphasis on procreation as an end of sexual intercourse reinforces the view of the order imposed on the passions.

The concern with ordered relationships, whether it is of parts to the whole, of an individual act to the sum total of a person's acts, or of humans to God, is characteristic of both *Humanae Vitae* and *Donum Vitae,* as seen above. I suggest that the structure of Catholic moral arguments on contraception and assisted reproduction are all concerned, at least to some extent, with ordered relationships. I explore these through three specific ordered relationships that structure Catholic thought on these issues; 1) object, intention, and circumstance; 2) the inseparability of the two ends of marital sexual acts; and 3) the principle of totality. These three elements do not represent altogether different arguments; they overlap in significant ways and are most coherent when viewed as a whole.

Object, Intention, and Circumstance

There is a widely held perception that the reason for Catholic prohibitions against most contraception is concern about the artificial nature of the interventions (e.g., contraceptive pill, condom, diaphragm). The fact that the Church allows the intentional avoidance of pregnancies through recourse to a woman's ovulatory cycle (the rhythm method) strengthens this perception.[27] In the case of reproductive technologies, one might believe that the Catholic Church's anti-technology bias is the reason it rejects these interventions. In both cases, there is a presumption that the Catholic Church is somehow anti-modern and old-fashioned—unwilling to accept new technology and information about reproduction. While there is some evidence to support this view, the magisterium has, for the most part, been clear in its support of medical, scientific, and technological progress. In fact, most of the arguments behind these moral prohibitions focus on different issues. These issues concern a certain understanding of the natural that is different and more complex than an outright technophobia.

For example in *Humanae Vitae,* the sexual act is understood as a natural act with "a decisive finality located in biological facticity" (McCormick 1989, 214). According to this view, the finality of sexual acts is not measured on the basis of procreative results. Rather, the critical factor is the performance of the act in a way that does not impede its ability to produce the desired result. The necessary condition of a natural act is that it is performed in a way that mirrors the ideal (or perfect) act. An emphasis on the completion and perfection of acts is consistent with the teleological framework of Catholic moral theology.

In addition to the metaphors of integrity and completion, which suggest a proper ordering of parts to the whole, the arguments about morality and the natural also invoke another image. For an action to be deemed morally good, the object, intention, and circumstance must be in proper alignment. These three components of moral action are central to Catholic morality: "The object, the intention, and the circumstances make up the 'sources,' or constitutive elements, of the morality of human acts" (United States Catholic Conference 1994, 1749). If we think about sex and procreation in the context of this description of moral actions, the following are two possible combinations:

	Object/Act	Intention/End	Circumstance
A.	Sexual intercourse with use of contraception	pleasure/nonprocreative	married couple
B.	Generation of life with assisted reproduction	procreation	married couple/ infertility

A and B represent the two combinations that Catholic teaching forbids. In case A, the intention is not the problem, since a couple can have sex that they intend to be nonprocreative (in the case of natural family planning) and remain within moral bounds. The locus of the moral problem is the object/act, especially when combined with the particular intention listed under A. The circumstances, in this case, have little bearing on moral judgments about the object. The fact that the couple is married justifies the use of sex but not of contraception. Thus, in case A, according to Catholic teaching, the object is intrinsically evil, especially when combined with that particular intention. Intrinsically evil acts cannot be mitigated by intentions or circumstances.

In case B, the problem lies with the object/act, even though the intention itself is desirable. To intend procreation is good, but the means are considered illicit because nonsexual acts are not an adequate locus for procreation. Every act of procreation must mirror God's original creative act. The sanctity of procreation is compromised when the generation of life is not the direct result of the mutual self-gift entailed in sexual acts. The intention in this case is not sufficient to justify the act; it must be combined with the proper sort of act. It is worth noting that the description of the object in A and B includes a limited description of the circumstance. In A, the act is sexual intercourse and the limiting circumstance is the use of contraception. In B, the act is the generation of life, limited by the use of assisted reproduction. This observation is an important element of the criticism that some Catholic theologians have leveled against the magisterium's insistence that these acts are intrinsically evil.

Two other combinations are possible:

	Object/Act	Intention/End	Circumstances
C.	Sexual intercourse	procreation	married couple/able to conceive
D.	Sexual intercourse	procreation	married couple/infertile

In case C, the act is sexual and the intention is procreative. The openness to procreation provides adequate justification for the sexual act. According to the Catholic tradition, the sex act needs justification to satisfy God's order. Procreation through sex maintains this important connection between the natural and the supernatural. Case C is the ideal sex act; act, intention, and circumstance are in perfect alignment.

Case D is a bit more problematic; in fact, it has been the topic of much writing about sexuality and contraception in the Catholic tradition. It concerns not only infertile couples but also couples who are beyond childbearing age. If procreation is the primary goal of marital sexual acts, how then can the Church consider acts that cannot possibly lead to the propagation of offspring permissible? The 1983 Code of Canon Law considers sterile marriages legitimate, while it views impotence as grounds for annulment.[28] Indeed, John Noonan considers the permissibility of so-called sterile marriages to be a weak point in the "pure procreative theory of intercourse"—the theory that the majority of theologians throughout Catholic history have espoused

(Noonan 1966, 290). He draws attention to the inconsistent response of the main strand of the tradition to "the marriage of the impotent" and the "marriage of the sterile" discussed earlier in this volume. This leads Noonan to question whether the theory of procreation as the only legitimate purpose of sexual intercourse is in fact immutable. In the case of impotence, the married couple's inability to engage in sexual intercourse is understood as a violation of the sacramental union between husband and wife, whereas sterile couples can engage in intercourse but with no possibility of achieving the good of offspring. As Noonan points out, "[I]f marriage was permissible without the goal of offspring, was nonprocreative intercourse possible" (291)?

Problems can emerge from this requirement of the alignment of object, intention, and circumstance. A clear example is the Catholic discussion about intrinsically evil acts. The magisterial prohibitions against artificial contraception and assisted reproduction invoke this language of intrinsic evil. To say that an act is intrinsically evil is to say that it is evil in an absolute sense; no circumstance or intention can make it good because choosing it "entails a disorder of the will" (United States Catholic Conference 1994, 1755). In other words, the will is not directed to the proper object. We have already noted that for Catholics, circumstance, intention, and object constitute the elements of the morality of human acts. All three of these elements must be good for the act itself to be judged morally good. While there is an apparent equality in importance of all three of these elements, the object has a slightly higher status, a point the catechism makes clear: "The *object of choice* can by itself vitiate an act in its entirety" (1755), and "The *circumstances* including the consequences, are secondary elements of a moral act" (1754). The catechism defines the object as the matter of a human act, or as the chosen good toward which the will directs itself. So, for example, a woman decides to begin taking the birth-control pill after having had four children because she develops a condition whereby another pregnancy could threaten her life. In this case, the object is contraception (impeding the possibility of conception), the intention is to protect her life, and the circumstance is that another pregnancy might be fatal in view of her physical condition.

If we examine this case, it might appear to some that the intention and the circumstances suggest legitimate reasons to pursue the act of avoiding pregnancy through contraception. The problem, according to the principle of intrinsically evil acts, is that a disordered will pursues contraceptive acts. In other words, the will has not chosen the proper act or object. Consequently, contraceptive acts are objectively evil—no circumstance or intention can ever change the objective nature of their evil. Richard McBrien describes this "three source theory" as serving the purpose of defending against utilitarian justifications that hold "that if the end results in a greater good, it can justify any acts or means (e.g., dropping a nuclear bomb on civilian populations in order to end a war)" (McBrien 1994, 966).

This matter of intrinsically evil acts has led to heated debates in Catholic moral theology. Some theologians, especially in the post–Vatican II era, have argued that the concept of intrinsically evil acts is not applied consistently in all areas of morality. So, for example, contraception is always intrinsically evil but killing is not; it can be justified in cases of self-defense and war. In other words, intentions and circumstances do alter the nature of the object—killing. Or, put differently, intentions and circumstances are often smuggled into the determination that an act is intrinsically evil. As we saw earlier in this chapter, the question about the intrinsic evil of contraception was a central concern of the Papal Birth Control Commission. The commission report used the distinction between physical and moral evil as a way to address the problem of intrinsic evil. In essence, the report claimed that by acknowledging the existence of physical evil in the world and in every action, moral discernment requires choosing the action that "carries with it the least possible negative element, according to the concrete situation of the couple" (McClory 1995, 182).

Theologians who have questioned the principle of intrinsically evil acts have been given a variety of labels, such as revisionists or proportionalists.[29] Cahill offers one description of this view. She writes that the real issue for this group is "exactly what constitutes a 'moral' evil. Perhaps some of the acts traditionally called 'intrinsic evils' are evil only in a limited sense, in the sense of being compromises with imperfect or tragic circumstances" (Cahill and Shannon 1968, 111). The contraception debate in the 1960s certainly propelled this discussion to prominence, but the same concerns raised about the supposed "intrinsic evils" of contraception are also applied to assisted reproduction.

"The Inseparable Connection"

The teleological nature of physical acts limits the acceptable combinations of the means and ends of procreation, so that procreative acts must be sexual and sexual acts must be procreative, or at least they must not intentionally prevent procreation. Since the 1960s, Catholic documents have framed this binary argument in the language of the inseparability of the unitive and procreative meanings of sexual acts. This notion of inseparability has been a significant component of the Catholic arguments against contraception and assisted reproduction. Furthermore, it evokes the metaphors of order and alignment—what I have identified as the interpretive key to Catholic teachings on sexual ethics. The unitive refers to the significance of sex as a reciprocal act of love and the procreative to the capacity of sex to generate new life. For the authors of *Donum Vitae,* these two meanings of sexuality coincide with the corporeal and spiritual dimensions of the sexual act.

Paul VI's encyclical letter *Humanae Vitae* was the first official articulation of the concept of inseparability of ends. In the letter, he writes:

> That teaching [that every marriage act must remain open to the transmission of life], often set forth by the magisterium, is founded upon the inseparable connection, willed by God and unable to be broken by man on his own initiative, between the two meanings of the conjugal act: the unitive meaning and the procreative meaning. Indeed, by its intimate structure, the conjugal act, while most closely uniting husband and wife, capacitates them for the generation of new lives, according to laws inscribed in the very being of man and woman. (Paul VI 1968, par. 12)

This passage indicates a pronounced shift, both in language and in overall approach, from the earlier Catholic tradition that insisted on procreation as the primary end of marriage.[30] Furthermore, the language of "ends" is replaced with the language of "meanings," a change that can be attributed to the influence of personalism in Catholic theology.[31] Meanings are more person-centered (persons ascribe meaning to acts) and more focused on process; ends, by contrast, are more act-centered and describe the outcome of a process or act. In addition to the linguistic change, the end of procreation is now made coequal with the end of unity of husband and wife. The spousal unity is meant to capture the "true mutual love" that is an intrinsic quality of properly ordered love and hence of properly ordered sexual acts. Not only does this approach give the unitive and the procreative equal status as meanings, it also deems them inseparable. This inseparability is sometimes described in terms of symbolic unity. Maura Ryan refers to the "symbolic unity of marriage, sexual intercourse and procreation" as a central component of the Catholic opposition to assisted reproduction (Ryan 2001, 46).

The notion of inseparability emerges from the naturalistic vision that claims that the conjugal act has an "intimate structure" that unites husband and wife and "capacitates them for the generation of new lives, according to laws inscribed in the very being of man and woman" (Paul VI 1968, par. 12). In other words, the act of intercourse, by its very nature, provides physical proof of these two meanings and their ontological connection. The noteworthy shift is not simply that the two ends are now viewed as equal; rather, it is the claim of their inseparability. This claim makes this argument useful in the evaluation of both contraception and assisted reproduction; mere equality of ends could not function as a convincing argument against assisted reproduction, whereas inseparability can. *Donum Vitae* highlights the inseparability argument. In fact, the authors remark that homologous artificial insemination "objectively effects an *analogous separation* between the goods and the meanings of marriage" (Congregation for the Doctrine of Faith 1987, II.B.4; emphasis mine). By this, they mean analogous to the separation that occurs when couples use artificial contraception.

Humanae Vitae claims that the connection between the two meanings, while "willed by God," is not hidden from humans; human reason can grasp it fully. According to the encyclical, this truth is eminently reasonable because "the design constitutive of marriage" which results in the transmission of life is visible and observable to all humans. "[O]ne who reflects well" would recognize that even a "reciprocal act of love" (one that expresses the unitive aspect of sex) when deliberately deprived of its life-transmitting potential has two consequences: it is in contradiction "with the design constitutive of marriage" and "with the will of the Author of life" (Paul VI 1968, par. 13). The pope appeals both to the natural and the supernatural; the unity is therefore not only between the two meanings of the conjugal act but also between the natural and the divine laws.

God's design for the generation of life is embedded in physical reality—its truths are "inscribed in the very being of man and woman" (par. 12). In his commentaries on *Humanae Vitae,* John Paul II refers to these embodied inscriptions as the language and theology of the body. He argues that from the fundamental structure of the marital act we discover that there are two "significances" (unitive and procreative) and that these two are connected inseparably. The fundamental structure reveals the meanings of the act by determining the act's purposes. This explains how we know the two purposes. That they are inseparably connected, however, is a bit more difficult to discern, at least from the perspective of the act's structure.[32] In the case of sex within marriage, John Paul II (echoing Paul VI) claims that each act unites husband and wife and makes possible the generation of new human life. In his view, this confirms the existence of the two significances. He claims that since both the unitive and procreative dimensions happen "through the fundamental structure," "it follows that the human person (with the necessity proper to reason, logical necessity) must read at the same time" the two significances as well as their inseparable connection (John Paul II 1997, 387–388). What I take John Paul II to be saying is that the unitive and procreative are inseparable because they achieve both ends by means of the same act. Inseparable in this sense means that the very structure of sexual intercourse is both unitive and procreative, at least to the extent of being open to procreation.

In another passage, John Paul II draws the connections between the fundamental structure of the act and the inseparability of meanings in a slightly different way. He claims that both manifest the divine plan or, using *Humanae Vitae*'s language, both are in "conformity with God's creative intention" (394). To separate these two meanings is to violate "the interior order of the conjugal union, which is rooted in the very order of the person" (398). He describes that inner order as self-control and self-mastery. He writes, "Man is precisely a person because he is a master of himself and has self-control" (398). Self-mastery is a concept that grounds self-gift, the term John Paul II uses to convey the subjective element of the conjugal act. In other words, in order to give oneself to the other in marriage, the spouse must be free of constraints that would make it difficult to experience "a communion of persons" (398).

When we transpose this argument about inseparability to the specific moral issues of contraception and assisted reproduction, we reach the following conclusion: the actions involved in both these issues require a deliberate interference with the fundamental structure of the sexual act that essentially allows a person to experience only one meaning. In the case of contraception, it blocks the procreative aspect while allowing the experience of the unitive, and in the case of assisted reproduction the unitive is not necessary for achieving the procreative end. John Paul II takes the argument even farther by suggesting that even the unitive meaning that appears to be experienced is somehow compromised.

For instance, John Paul II rejects the notion in the case of contraception that couples engaged in sex experience the unitive meaning fully. He claims that while in an empirical sense the unitive aspect is experienced ("a real bodily union is carried out in the conjugal act"), it is not an experience that reflects the "interior truth and dignity of personal communion" (398). In essence, the intentional obstruction of fecundity negates the full significance of the unitive aspect. For the unitive aspect to reflect the objective truth of the conjugal act, it cannot be separated from its procreative capacity. In assisted reproductive technologies, procreative capacity is enhanced or assisted. The particular act necessary to produce a child, however, is not sexual and is therefore devoid of any unitive meaning, according to Catholic teaching—it lacks the fundamental structures through which couples are able to experience the unitive meaning of the act.

It seems worth noting that these discussions of the significance or meaning of sexual acts do not draw on the experiences of the persons involved. In other words, that a couple using contraceptive measures might feel that the unitive aspect of their relationship is enhanced is not part of the theological discussion of marriage.[33] Similarly, using assisted reproduction to have a child might increase what the married couple believes to be the unitive aspect of their sexual relationship. Does viewing sex only in terms of its "fundamental structures" capture the experience of sex? Defenders of church teaching might respond that knowledge of these significances does come from experience and that the principle of inseparability is knowable from reflection on the structure of the sexual act. Such a debate might reveal quite starkly the slippery nature of appeals to experience.[34]

Of course, the lack of attention to human experience makes sense when one understands the inseparability argument as profoundly embedded in the sacramental theology of marriage. Sexual intercourse in marriage enacts a larger set of relationships with the sacred. While John Paul II refers to the "interior truth" and "dignity of personal communion," the ultimate communion is the sacramental bond with God. In the encyclical *Familiaris Consortio*, John Paul II summarizes the various elements of the Catholic teaching on inseparability. He claims that when couples use contraception to separate

> these two meanings that God the Creator has inscribed in the being of man and woman and in the dynamism of their sexual communion, they act as "arbiters" of the divine plan and they "manipulate" and degrade human sexuality—and with it themselves and their married partner—by altering the value of "total" self-giving. Thus the innate language that expresses the total reciprocal self-giving of husband and wife is overlaid, through contraception, by an objectively contradictory language, namely, that of not giving oneself totally to the other. (John Paul II 1981, 32)

In this passage, John Paul II claims that separating the two meanings causes harms in three distinct ways. First, it harms the individual's relationship to God by attempting to usurp God's power; the transmission of life is part of the divine plan and human interference is a sign of pride. Second, there is harm to the marriage partner since the sexual act is intended to be a total gift of self and the use of contraception, according to the encyclical, represents a contradictory act. Third, a violation of meanings that are "inscribed in the being" of the person degrades the self. Once again we see how Catholic doctrine appeals to the three dimensions of order: the supernatural/natural order, the social order, and the interior order.

The emphasis on the inseparability of meanings shifts the attention away from procreation as the primary good to a discussion of the most appropriate means for achieving this end. By raising the value of the unitive aspect to an equal level, Paul VI achieved two things; he kept the value of procreation intact and he acknowledged that sex has other effects. The practical upshot of this shift is an expansion of the meaning of sex to two coequal meanings instead of one end. However, by insisting on the essential inseparability of these two meanings, Catholic doctrine imposes another limitation. This limitation is most evident in the area of assisted reproduction, where having procreation as the only goal is not sufficient. Put differently, the morality of assisted reproduction does not entail the justification of a sex act since in most cases a sex act is not requisite. So while the debate about contraception must explore the meaning and "fundamental structure" of the sexual act, the debate about assisted reproduction does not, or at least that is not necessarily entailed. Instead, one must explore the issue of human interference with reproduction, and since reproduction is understood theologically as willed by God, we can see how this argument about inseparability reflects the order of the natural to the supernatural.

Principle of Totality

In the previous two sections, I described ways to characterize the structure of the arguments, and I suggested that their concern with order is notable. The moral order is exemplified in one way by the doctrine of the sources of morality: the relations of intention to object to circumstance. Moral actions can only be evaluated in the context of a proper alignment between these parts. The cosmic order, or the relation of the natural to the supernatural, is captured in the arguments about the inseparability of ends. The connection between the unitive and procreative meanings of conjugal sexual acts reflects God's participation in procreation and the sacred character of such acts. Finally, the metaphor of order also has a strongly physical aspect, and the principle of totality captures that aspect.

As we have seen in the discussions of *Humanae Vitae* and *Donum Vitae,* the natural law grounds a view of the natural that is connected to the proper physical execution of acts—an emphasis on the fundamental structure of acts. Thus, a natural act is one that is allowed to achieve its goal unimpeded. The act that achieves its goal or at least *can* achieve its goal is complete and whole. On the basis of this reasoning, the principle of totality, the idea that one may legitimately sacrifice the good of the part for the good of the whole, might appear contradictory, especially if one understands the components of the act as parts, since the logic of totality would suggest that the intention or circumstance could mitigate the object of the act.

Catholic moral theology has applied this principle to a variety of entities: the physical body, the person as a whole, and society as a body. Proponents of change in Catholic teaching have tried to apply it to the relationship of the act to the whole of a person's life. However, the magisterium has also utilized it to support the prohibition against contraception. For instance, the principle of totality plays an important role in the structure of *Humanae Vitae,* where Pope Paul VI rejects its (incorrect) use in arguments for artificial contraception and uses it to bolster his own argument against artificial contraception.

Pius XI first introduced the principle in the modern era in 1930, when he applied it to the human organism. In the intervening years, it has come to symbolize divisions in the understanding of moral justification in Catholicism. The range of applications essentially correlates to whether the whole under consideration is the human body or, in Gerard Hughes's terms, "nonorganic wholes such as the family, the state, or society at large" (Hughes 1986, 629). This controversy about the proper application of the principle of totality is related to conflicting views about the moral significance of the category "natural." Natural, in everyday usage, implies wholesomeness and purity. Totality, when applied to the human organism, captures this sense of the natural. The theological implications of the natural as complete or intact stem from the belief that creation is part of God's divine plan. In this view, the wholeness and completion of actions that involve the human body must correlate to this divine plan. In fact, the natural involves a kind of biological integrity and perfection. By contrast, many revisionist theologians have expanded the object of totality to include the sorts of nonorganic wholes mentioned by Hughes. In that context, the sense of natural as complete and perfect is turned into something quite different. Instead of a single body, the emphasis is on the relationships between entities. The more-limited definition of totality as bodily integrity implies that God's created order is perfect and complete. The broader interpretation where totality describes the integrity of a relationship suggests that God's creation is evolving. In this interpretation, totality can best be explained as balance.

We see this most vividly in Paul VI's encyclical on birth control, where he rehearses the arguments in favor of changing the Catholic teaching on contraception. He singles out the claim that the principle of totality implies that one should not evaluate individual sexual acts in marriage apart from the ensemble of marital acts. This is a use of the principle of totality where the organism is the marriage itself. Paul VI rejects this appeal to totality but later in the encyclical uses totality in a different sense to support his claim that there are limits to human domination over the "body and its functions; limits which no man, whether a private individual or one invested with authority, may licitly surpass." The principle of totality understood as "the integrity of the human organism and its functions" provides the key for determining those limits (Paul VI 1968, par. 17). The metaphor of integrity suggests a biological wholeness which, according to this view, is a characteristic of human functions. Thus, interfering with the integrity of an act is tantamount to an irresponsible exercise of human dominion over nature. In the context of this interpretation, the relationship of the parts to the whole is the relationship of every aspect of the performance of a physical act to its overall purpose. Sexual acts have a divinely ordained purpose, and tinkering with the parts of such acts is a violation not only of the natural law but also of the divine law. More important, in *Humanae Vitae,* Paul VI rejects an interpretation of the principle of the totality where the totality is anything other than the human organism. Many critics of *Humanae Vitae* and *Donum Vitae* have argued on the basis of the principle of totality that it is difficult to properly evaluate acts (parts) apart from circumstances (the totality). The more traditional view would claim that the totality is the act itself. Such a view bolsters the argument that certain acts can be intrinsically evil.

Pius XI originally used the principle in *Casti Connubii* to apply to eugenic uses of sterilization.[35] In arguing against sterilization, he appeals to Christian doctrine and the light of human reason to support this logic of totality. He writes that

> private individuals have no power over the members of their bodies than that which pertains to their natural ends; and they are not free to destroy or mutilate their members, or in any other way render themselves unfit for their natural functions, except when no other provision can be made for the good of the whole body. (Pius XI 1968, 36)

Pius XI's articulation of this principle is consistent with Catholic natural law as it pertains to bodies and their natural functions. The final part of the statement provides room for an exception as a last resort for "the good of the whole body." It appears, however, that he understands the whole body in its organic, physical sense. In the post–Vatican II era, moral theologians as well as the magisterium have embraced a personalistic understanding of the whole body that would equate the body with the person.

A clear example of this understanding is in John Paul II's encyclical letter *Veritatis Splendor*. He is responding to what he calls "objections of physicalism and naturalism" to the Church's use of natural law reasoning. He interprets this critique by Catholic theologians as an attempt "to dissociate" the moral acts from the bodily dimension of its exercise" (John Paul II 1993, par. 49). He responds to them by affirming the inseparability of body and soul and by cementing the connection between that view and the natural law. He writes that the natural law "refers to man's proper and primordial nature, the 'nature of the human person' which is *the person himself in the unity of soul and body*" (par. 50). Then, quoting both *Humanae Vitae* and *Donum Vitae,* he offers a definition of the natural law as the "rational order" that governs the person's response to the creation—an order that the direction and regulation of life and actions, especially the use of the human body, exemplify. For John Paul II, physical acts are expressions of the person as "unified totality." The body and the human person are virtually synonymous, and natural inclinations are judged by their relationship to the "human person and his [*sic*] authentic fulfillment" (par. 50).

In an interesting twist, John Mahoney uses the principle of totality to describe the direction of contemporary Catholic moral theology and in doing so succeeds in capturing the controversy about the principle's application. His discussion of the principle of totality as a metaphor draws attention to the centrality of ordered relationships in Catholic debates about contraception and assisted reproduction. He makes this explicit by noting the connection between the principle and both St. Augustine's and Thomas Aquinas's notions of order. Mahoney bases his constructive proposal for Catholic moral theology on what he identifies as two features of the recent period of renewal: a drive toward totality and an attempt to recognize diversity (Mahoney 1987, 302). Mahoney writes, "Much of recent moral theology can be viewed as a bid to recover or to reclaim the living unity which links and subsumes all this into an intelligible whole which can easily be lost to view in the short-sighted peering at the parts" (310).

The sources of morality, inseparability, and totality are significant components of the Catholic arguments about contraception and assisted reproduction. Furthermore, they all evoke the metaphors of order and alignment—what I have identified as the interpretive key to Catholic teachings on sexual ethics. An alignment of a different sort also pervades Catholic teachings on marriage and reproduction. It involves the proper relationship of male to female and ultimately of biological sex to gender roles. We turn to the "order of gender" in the next chapter.

4 GENDER

From our exploration of the normative Catholic teachings on marriage and reproduction, we can conclude the following: the Catholic tradition holds procreation as a good but not an absolute one. It is circumscribed by the relationship between (married) male and female and by the nature of the act that leads to procreation (sexual intercourse between male and female). Marriage, as we saw, maintains order in several relationships. In this context, the discourse on sexuality also becomes a discourse about gender. Marriage is premised on an understanding of male and female as separate and distinct yet complementary and connected to specific biological sex traits. This particular view of male and female is the basis of both the definitions of morally legitimate sexual partners and morally legitimate sexual acts.

Debates about contraception and assisted reproduction, particularly as they relate to consistency and change in moral doctrine, lead to some broader questions: Is the Church adapting the content of its teachings to modernity or is it simply rearticulating existing teachings in language more suitable to the era? Regardless of the answer, the theological and ethical arguments that govern sexual behavior do more than simply tell Catholics how to conduct their sexual and reproductive activities; they also reinforce a scheme of complementary gender roles intended to maintain the proper order between the sexes that Catholicism believes supports the whole of God's created order. Teachings about marriage and reproduction reaffirm the significance of the complementarity view and might lead one to believe that gender complementarity captures the whole of the Catholic view about gender and sex. It would be a mistake, in my view, to stop our inquiry into gender and sex in Catholicism with this model. To do so would leave us with an impoverished picture of the tradition that fails to grasp complexities and ambiguities about male/female relations and what those relations imply about power structures in both the public and private sphere.

Hence, we must look for other clues about gender in these documents. One significant source is the metaphorical language official Catholic documents employ to characterize the Church as female.[1] For example, these documents often describe the relationship of Christ and the Church metaphorically as a marriage between a male Christ and a female Church. While this "marriage" is intended as a metaphor, I think it reveals Catholic views about authority and about the feminine role. It represents a template for relationships between human men and women.[2] The documents are explicit in suggesting that since the Church is a bride, a mother, and a virgin, brides, mothers, and virgins ought to be like the Church. These images provide a rich resource for understanding the relationship of gender to sexual ethics. Aligning feminine roles with the institutional Church raises questions both about what it means to be female and what it means to be the Church. The images function as a point where attitudes about gender, sex, and authority converge.

AN INTERESTING SYMMETRY

When Pope Paul VI issued his encyclical letter *Humanae Vitae* in 1968, he reiterated the traditional ban on contraception but offered seemingly new arguments that reflected a more sympathetic attitude to the positive role of sexual pleasure and fulfillment in marriage or, at the very least, expanded on the meaning of marital sexuality.[3] This new attitude emerged from the personalist criteria that emphasize the dignity of the human person. Pope Paul VI raised sexual intimacy to an equal status with procreation as ends or purposes of conjugal sex, but he constrained this equality by requiring inseparability. By claiming that these two ends were inseparable, he ensured that equality would be grounded in a relationship of dependence; neither end can be satisfied unless the other end is satisfied as well. This revised way of evaluating the morality of sexual acts moves from a hierarchical model of ends to a model of interdependence between ends. Joseph Selling comments on this innovation by noting that "one finds no evidence of a teaching before *Humanae Vitae* that proposes a 'twofold meaning' (*significations*) for marital intercourse—neither in this century nor in the previous ones" (Selling 1998, 26).

The principle of inseparability mirrors (at least in a structural sense) the prominent Catholic doctrine of gender complementarity. Fulfillment for male and female persons comes from their complementary interaction. They are equal but not independent from each other.[4] Like the ends of marriage, each "completes" the other.[5] What does this conceptual connection between gender complementarity and inseparability of ends reveal about the Catholic ethics of sex and its politics of gender?

Deposing a hierarchical model was necessary for the Church's attempts to respond to forces outside and within the Church that were pushing for changes in the ethics of sex and gender. The Church responded with a teaching that each entity, whether gender (in the case of complementarity) or the ends of conjugal sex (in the case of the inseparability of ends), had equal value. But by characterizing the bond itself as a relationship of dependence, the new, more equitable model reinforced the preexisting moral and theological positions. In the new models, the binary of gender and the dualism of ends were still in an unequal relationship.

Gender complementarity and the inseparability of ends share more than an interesting structural symmetry. Their development occurred almost simultaneously in the history of Catholic moral theology. It was during the Vatican II era that both relationships underwent a similar conceptual shift from a more hierarchical model to one based on greater equity. As a result of Vatican II's insistence that the dignity of the human person is central to the evaluation of moral actions, any view that derived moral norms from a static, physical view of nature became suspect. The magisterium had to revise the view that procreation is the primary inherent end of sex and the view that the male gender is inherently superior to the female. They replaced both views with an emphasis on equality of ends and of genders.[6]

The configuration of gender relations in Catholicism is certainly relevant to the evaluation of sexual practices, as John Paul II makes explicit in the following passage:

> *Respect for the two meanings of the conjugal act can develop fully only on the basis of a profound reference to the personal dignity of what in the human person*

is intrinsic to masculinity and femininity, and inseparably in reference to the
personal dignity of the new life, which can result from the conjugal union of the
man and the woman. (John Paul II 1997, 416)

While some aspects of this passage are opaque, it does draw explicit attention to the perceived symbiotic relationship between inherent gender characteristics and the inseparability of ends.

GENDER COMPLEMENTARITY

The implications of the symmetry between inseparability and complementarity become clearer when one explores the doctrine of gender complementarity in more detail. Proponents of this doctrine begin with the presupposition that male and female are essential and stable genders that exist in a binary opposition. They believe that gender is determined exclusively on the basis of biological sexual characteristics and that identity is firmly grounded in gender assignment; thus, each person lives and experiences his or her identity as male or female. Gender complementarity does not simply tell us about the meaning of gender; it also dictates the appropriate form of relationship that can exist between the genders. That relationship is based on difference. It conveys a sense of the purpose of each gender: each gender is to complement its opposite.

The verb "to complement" means both to supply mutual needs and offset mutual lacks. This dual definition highlights both the positive and negative aspects of the complementarity model of gender relations. It suggests more positively that the two parties (male and female) are helping each other—providing what the other cannot provide. This is clearly derived from a biological model of reproduction where the male and female each contribute to the process of reproduction. Their contributions are not identical or necessarily equal in a strict sense. What is equal is the *necessity* of each contribution.

The aspect of the definition that focuses on offsetting mutual lacks gestures toward the more problematic aspect of the gender complementarity model. This model seems fair and equitable, but the reality is that most Catholic writings on sexual ethics emphasize the female lack. Put more directly, while an ideal view is of gender complementarity as a balance with each side serving the other, Catholic documents often draw it as a hierarchy. It is hierarchical not so much in the sense that one party submits to the other but rather that the designated role for the female gender is one that is inherently more repressive; they often define the female primarily in terms of her role as complement to the male, as his helper. Ross describes the characteristics assigned to each gender as follows: receptivity and maternal nurturing are female qualities, and initiation and activity are male qualities.[7]

An earlier and much stronger incarnation of the complementarity model existed in the pre–Vatican II period.[8] Like this contemporary model, it claimed an equality of rights and insisted that each gender had a specified natural role that complemented the other. It differed, however, because it insisted that the equality of rights did not necessarily apply in the realm of marriage and family. Leo XIII's *Arcanum,* the document that we identified as the starting point of modern Catholic sexual ethics, is explicit in its view of a strong gender complementarity. The discussion of gender relations appears in the context of the overall trajectory of Leo's encyclical letter on marriage. He traces the development of the institution of marriage, especially the "relief and remedy" to pagan marriage that Christianity provides. Christ renewed matrimony and made it a sacrament. As a result, "the rights of husband and wife have been equalized"; "the dignity of woman has been asserted and vindicated" (Liebard 1978, 7). Nevertheless, the husband is the head and chief of the family; the wife "should be subject to and obey the man, not as a servant, but as a companion; and so neither honor nor dignity is lost by the rendering of obedience" (6). This version of gender complementarity emphasizes a hierarchy between male and female. Later magisterial writings place less emphasis on woman's subjugation to man and more on sex-role stereotyping, a characteristic of a weaker version of gender complementarity.

Like Leo XIII, Pius XI is quite explicit in his support of a strong hierarchical complementarity. While he tells women to submit to the headship of their husbands, he also reminds them that such subjection does "not deny or take away the liberty which fully belongs to the woman both in view of her dignity as a human person, and in view of her most noble office as wife and mother and companion" (Pius XI 1930, 15). He cautions women against "exaggerated liberty": "For if the man is the head, the woman is the heart, and as he occupies the chief place in ruling, so she may and ought to claim for herself the chief place in love" (15). We see in this passage the basic elements of complementarity; equal dignity and sex-role stereotyping. The element of subjection and obedience to the husband represents the strong form of this version of the doctrine.

More than a decade later, in an address to members of the Federation of Italian Women on a pilgrimage to the Shrine of Loretto, Pope Pius XII elaborated the Church's understanding of male-female relations. In this address, he defines complementarity, its origin, and its implications. Although he intends to promote the dignity of women by pushing for its equality to the dignity of men, he continues to describe women as secondary to men in some ways (helpers) but superior to men in other ways. Women's attributes, especially their suitability for motherhood, are inherent and essential, he argues.

He begins by expressing his happiness that the Federation of Women has invited him to address them at the Shrine of Loretto, the preserved site of the Virgin Mary's home in Nazareth that was transported miraculously to Loretto, Italy. The location is significant because it allows him to draw the connection between the Church's doctrine of complementarity and the Virgin Mary. He exclaims that Mary's "lofty example might teach [all women] the secret of all greatness" (Liebard 1978, 180). The fact that the Church proposes Mary "as the sublime model of a Virgin and a Mother" indicates, in his view, "the high esteem that Christianity nourishes for womanhood and the immense trust which the Church herself rests in woman's power for good and her mission on behalf of the family and society" (181). In typically flowery prose, he describes woman as the "crown of creation, and in a certain sense its masterpiece . . . that gentle creature, to whose delicate hands God seems to have entrusted the future of the world to such a great extent, insofar as she is man's helper" (181). Pius XII highlights one aspect of complementarity here—the association of women with goodness and delicacy. He gives woman an important responsibility but defines it in the context of her relationship to man as his helper.

In this important speech, Pius XII denies that the Church opposes women's emancipation, or that it favors the oppression of women. Indeed, he goes to great lengths to associate the oppression of women with paganism ("that unjust status of personal inferiority to which paganism often condemned women" [183]). He defends the Church as a champion for women's rights, especially as a protector of her dignity. She shares that dignity with man since both are God's creatures. According to Pius XII, it would be wrong to claim as Catholic the view that women are inferior or less valuable.

Piux XII claims that the relationship of complementarity exists because while God has created male and female to have the same destiny on earth (to fill the earth and subdue and rule over it), they have different functions "like two roads leading to the same destination" (184). The difference of functions can be seen in the different physical and psychological structures, but the differences are balanced "by the wonderful laws of compensation, and which fit together to lend a marvelous harmony to the work of each" (184). Then, in a clear articulation of the doctrine, he states that there is between male and female "an absolute equality in personal and fundamental values, but different functions, which are complementary and superbly equivalent, and from them arise the various rights and duties of the one and the other" (184). He argues that the primary function of woman is motherhood and that this is apparent from her physical and psychic structure. It is her mission and through it she can achieve her true perfection. Since not all women will become mothers, the pope uses motherhood metaphorically to describe an attitude—one that women can attain through other forms of sacrificing themselves for the sake of others.

Pope John Paul II has developed and expanded this doctrine more fully than any of his predecessors.[9] Most important, he has expanded on the philosophical and theological bases of gender complementarity. A quote from his 1995 *Letter to Women* captures the essence of this doctrine:

> *Woman complements man, just as man complements woman: Men and women are complementary. Womanhood expresses the "human" as much as manhood does, but in a different and complementary way. When the Book of Genesis speaks of "help," it is not referring merely to acting but also to being. Womanhood and manhood are complementary not only from the physical and psychological points of view, but also from the ontological. It is only through the duality of the "masculine" and the "feminine" that the "human" finds full realization. (John Paul II 1995b, 2)*

According to this view, gender roles are more than mere biological or psychological differences between male and female; they are necessary for human fulfillment. The identity of the human person as either masculine or feminine is coherent only as part of a duality. Each person's gender is inscribed on them in a biological sense but is also inscribed through them in their relations to the opposite gender.

John Paul II's interpretation of the Genesis story, especially the Yahwist account of the second chapter, reinforces this notion of gender as "primordially" inscribed.[10] Unlike the Priestly account of the first chapter of Genesis, where God creates male and female simultaneously, the Yahwist account describes the creation of man first. He is given "every beast of the field and every bird of the air" but still longs for a "helper fit for him." God responds by creating woman from man's rib. The pope interprets both creation accounts in the context of their appearance in Matthew 19 and Mark 10, the gospel passages where Jesus responds to the question from the Pharisees about the indissolubility of marriage. His response refers back to both Genesis accounts. The pope points out, "Jesus Christ referred twice to the beginning" (John Paul II 1997, 25). While he acknowledges that the Priestly account is chronologically later than the Yahwist, he describes it as "much more mature both as regards the image of God, and as regards the formulation of the essential truths about man" (28). Nevertheless, he chooses to focus his reflection on the more ancient Yahwist account, because in his view it is psychologically more profound.[11] Through "its primitive mythical character," we are able to extrapolate the subjective aspects of the creation of man. The separate creation of woman from man's rib in the second creation story suggests to the pope that what he calls "original solitude" preceded "original unity." He writes:

> The narrative of the first chapter of Genesis does not know the problem of man's original solitude. Man is "male and female" right from the beginning. On the contrary, the Yahwist text of the second chapter authorizes us, in a way, to think first only of the man since, by means of the body, he belongs to the visible world but goes beyond it. Then, it makes us think of the same man, but through the dualism of sex. (43)

By this he means that "corporality," the existence of the human body before the creation of woman from man's rib, is not to be identified completely with "sexuality," the distinction into male and female. The original solitude is a deeper structure in the person than the unity that occurs when man is granted a helper in the form of woman (43).[12] While God's act creates two separate beings, male and female, they exist in a unity—separate in their sex but unified in their humanity. Their humanity is a prior or, in the pope's language, a deeper part of the structure of personal subjectivity than is sexual identification. The deeper structure of the person is not gendered male or female, it is simultaneously male and female. Sexual intercourse enables male and female to become "one flesh," to catch a fleeting glimpse of their original solitude. In *Mulieres Dignitatem,* he emphasizes this "character of a union of persons" (the mutual relations between men and women) because it has existed from the very beginning and "has to correspond to the personal truth of their being" (John Paul II 1988, 23). Gender complementarity describes the order that ought to exist between male and female—an order that is necessary if unity is to be achieved.

The unity evident in Genesis expresses both a unified integrity in human nature and a duality that, in John Paul II's view, is an ontological necessity. The coming together of male and female in the conjugal/sexual act enacts the unity of the two genders in a physical way. That unity, however, is already present in the "deepest structures" of human subjectivity. It would seem that the language of the priority of humanity to gender identity would imply fairness—all persons are human beings before they are male or female—but in certain passages John Paul II's view of this problem reflects a different model. For instance, he writes, "As Genesis 2:23 already shows, femininity finds itself, in a sense, in the presence of masculinity, while masculinity is confirmed through femininity" (John Paul II 1997, 49). This passage states quite clearly that masculinity precedes femininity, since to be confirmed implies that masculinity already exists. By contrast, the activity of femininity finding itself conveys a different image. It suggests that without masculinity, consciousness of femininity would be impossible, whereas masculinity only needs femininity to confirm what it already knows. This coheres with the second Genesis account of creation where man exists before woman. John Paul II's interpretation of this passage, however, tries to suggest that what existed before woman was a nongendered entity. The state of original solitude is marked primarily by man's consciousness that he is different from the world of living beings. That consciousness gives rise to the need for a "helpmate" and ultimately to the relationship of complementarity that exists between male and female after the creation of woman.

John Paul II writes in *Mulieres Dignitatem* that women's roles are circumscribed by their biological capacity to reproduce and by their "naturally spousal predisposition." This predisposition comes from the realization that a person is a being "whom the creator from the beginning has willed for their own sake" (John Paul II 1988, par. 20). That person can only fully discover herself through the experience of giving herself to another. John Paul II writes that "in conceiving and giving birth to a child, the woman 'discovers herself through a sincere gift of self' " (par. 18).

In *Mulieres,* the pope is careful to distinguish woman's "bio-physiological" capacity for motherhood from her psychosocial capacities. He claims that "scientific analysis fully confirms that the very physical contribution of woman is naturally disposed to motherhood—conception, pregnancy, and giving birth" (par. 18). In this view, women's very physicality predisposes them to maternity. More controversial, however, is his claim that "motherhood *is linked to the personal structure of the woman and to the personal dimension of the gift*" (1988, par. 18). He expresses this notion more fully through the language of the "unique intuition" that inheres in women. The pope bases the difference between male and female not only on physical sexual attributes but also on something more abstract.

For example, in *Evangelium Vitae,* he claims that women have a special genius that comes from their experience of motherhood where they are involved in a special communion with the mystery of life. He writes, "This unique contact with the new human being developing within her gives rise to an attitude towards human beings not only towards her own child, but every human being, which profoundly marks the woman's personality. This is the fundamental contribution that the Church and humanity expect from women" (John Paul II 1995a, par. 99). On this view, gender, especially when it allows for the particular experience of maternity, defines women.

In *Mulieres,* he comments on Genesis again, drawing on the description of the Fall that indicates that man shall rule over woman. He stresses that man's domination of woman has occurred because of human sinfulness. John Paul II describes it as "a hereditary sinfulness" that issues in the constant "inclination to sin". The Genesis statement that "your desire shall be for your husband, and he shall rule over you" (Gen 3:16) not only harms women but also "diminishes the true dignity of the man" (John Paul II 1988, par. 10). The pope affirms women's right to oppose such oppression, but he is quick to add that such opposition "must not under any condition lead to the 'masculinization' of women" (par. 10). By that he means that while women are right to resist domination, they can only do so while retaining their essential femininity. He warns that in trying to break free from domination, women might "*deform and lose what constitutes their essential richness*" (par. 10). Complementarity, thus, has strict limits and boundaries. The pope asserts that "the personal resources of femininity are certainly no less than the resources of masculinity: they are merely different" (par. 10).

In John Paul II's view, receptivity and maternity are the qualities that constitute women's essential richness. He believes the ultimate model for women is the Virgin Mary, who best exemplifies these characteristics. "Virginity and motherhood coexist in her," he proclaims. These two "dimensions" are the "two paths in the vocation of women as persons" (par. 17). Both motherhood and virginity embody the spousal predisposition, which John Paul II describes using the metaphor of gift. Also noteworthy in light of the Marian model is his statement that "[t]he man—even with all his sharing in parenthood—always remains 'outside' the process of pregnancy and the baby's birth; in many ways he has to *learn* his own '*fatherhood*' *from the mother*" (par. 18). That the status of fatherhood is submissive to the maternal echoes the relationship captured in the metaphor of the Church as mother and teacher.

The issue of women's ordination has been one of the most significant applications of the doctrine of gender complementarity. The Church argues that since each sex has appropriate roles that emerge from their very natures and bodies, it is reasonable to exclude women from the priesthood. Women are prohibited from becoming priests on the basis of theological anthropology (Ross 1992, 113).[13] Thus, the role of priest is dictated by biology; physical structure imbues males with the capacity to be a priest—to hold a position of institutional power in the Church. These positions of power ensure that the human face of the Church is male, but the Vatican continues to insist (at least metaphorically) on the femininity of the Church.

Gender Theory and Feminist Responses to Gender Complementarity

Many theorists of gender have questioned the notion that such "a binary frame of thinking about gender," to use Judith Butler's language, could possibly be free of a repressive imposition of power. Thomas Laqueur's important historical work on sex and gender is one important perspective on the debate about the hierarchical power relations between male and female. Laqueur identifies two models for the relationship of male to female—the one-sex/one-flesh model and the two-sex/two-flesh model—and suggests that the latter is a more recent (post-Enlightenment) creation.

The older one-sex model developed from the view that there were two genders and that these genders corresponded to one sex. The difference between the genders was in degree, not in kind. Thus, while male and female genders exhibit differences, they were essentially two versions of one sex. For most who held this view, the one sex was the male sex, and the female biological manifestation was an imperfect or less-developed version of the male. Hence, there was no ontological difference between the male and female sexes. According to Laqueur, the difference between male and female "refer[red] not to the clear and distinct kinds of being we might mean when we speak of opposite sexes, but rather to delicate, difficult-to-read shadings of one sex" (Laqueur 1990, 52). Laqueur explains the one-sex model as the result of an incorrect biological understanding of the body.

The two-sex model, according to Laqueur, emerged around the time of the Enlightenment. Its primary influences were epistemological and sociohistorical factors rather than biological and scientific ones. He describes its emergence as follows: "Sometime in the eighteenth century, sex as we know it was invented. The reproductive organs went from being paradigmatic sites for displaying hierarchy resonant throughout the cosmos to being the foundation of incommensurable difference" (149). This utter separation between male and female transcended biology. Not only were male and female sexual organs deemed completely different, everything about the two genders was seen as opposite. Whereas the male body was the measure in the one-sex model, the female body, now viewed as ontologically distinct, became "the battleground for redefining the ancient, intimate, fundamental social relation: that of woman to man" (150). In the one-sex/one-flesh model, gender was what determined difference, since the physical facts of sex were seen as gradations of kind. Put differently, gender presuppositions played a role in constructing the explanations of male and female sexual difference. In the two-sex/two-flesh model, difference and opposition resided in genital structures first and foremost. Attitudes about gender followed from this biological distinction.

The shift that Laqueur traces corresponds to the rise of the gender-complementarity model which views the difference between male and female as an opposition grounded in an ontological reality—God's creative activity. This passage from the Pontifical Council for the Family stresses this connection: "[P]rofound respect must be maintained for the difference between man and woman which reflects the love and fruitfulness of God himself" (Pontifical Council for the Family 1995, par. 122). In the natural world, God orders his creation according to sexual difference. The relationship of male to female is complementary. The difference between them on this view is egalitarian, not hierarchical, or so it appears.

Susan Ross challenges the inequality of the complementarity model. She argues that John Paul II's model of complementarity is more accurately described as a model of dichotomy. Because the model stresses a strict separation of roles, it magnifies sexual differences between men and women. Ross quotes one theologian whose description of difference captures this point: "Difficult as it is to describe complementarity in adequate language, it may be seen from the vantage point of the marital act, or the reproductive act, as characterized by equal dignity and equally active participation but diversity of role." In Ross's view, this theologian focuses entirely on the moment of intercourse rather than on the larger context of reproduction, which includes nurturing, educating, and socializing the children that might result from the reproductive act (Ross 1992, 124). This reveals a central Catholic attitude: gender roles are closely connected to physical sexual capacities.[14]

In Ross's estimation, while the recent shift to personalism ought to have led to a complete rejection of natural law criteria, the particular brand of personalism embraced by church documents has been "appropriated by the natural law tradition" in such a way that it "permits personalism to assume a traditional configuration of gender differences, albeit on a 'subjective' rather than 'natural' basis" (Ross 1991, 360). She argues that contemporary Catholic teaching has embraced a personalism that retains vestiges of an outmoded gender theory based on a naturalistic view. She explains this blend of personalism and "natural law tradition" in a later article, where she compares the "phenomenologically influenced understandings" of modern theologians such as Hans Urs von Balthasar, Louis Bouyer, and John Paul II with traditional Thomistic and Augustinian theologies. The modern thinkers reject an explicit hierarchy between male and female but retain "an ontological distinction" between them. Ross points out that this ontological distinction rooted in nature leads to an analysis of the male as active source of generation and the female as passive recipient (Ross 1992, 112).

Ross's detailed exegesis of the concept of gender complementarity supports the conclusion reached by other Catholic feminist theologians. For instance, Mary Jo Weaver writes, "Official Catholic teaching about women—complementarity—is a religious form of sex-role stereotyping" (Weaver 1995, 50). She goes on to point out that the criticism by feminists is not directed at sexual difference per se but rather at "whether there are different human *natures* and whether 'different natures' dictate a divinely ordained and permanent division of labor among men and women" (51). Weaver's comments reflect the view expressed by many Catholic feminists about the hidden power dynamic of the complementarity model.

Christine Gudorf draws our attention to an example of that power dynamic; although Pope John Paul II's views represent a shift toward stressing the equality of women, much of his teaching "on the nature and role of women still demonstrates a romantic pedestalization of women" (Gudorf 1996, 70). The clearest evidence of this, in her view, is that the pope views motherhood as not simply one element of being a woman but rather as its essential defining feature. She notes that like the popes before him, John Paul II favors the view of maternity expressed in 1 Timothy 2:15 that motherhood offers women a way to salvation.[15] Gudorf is concerned about the centrality and pervasiveness of the connection between maternity, Mary, and essential femininity in contemporary Catholic views on women, marriage, and sexuality.

The Catholic Church holds a very particular gender relationship as ideal, and this view is the basis of most recent Catholic teaching on sexual ethics. Complementarity is the metaphor for describing both the difference between men and women and their proper relationship to each other. Since the Church conflates gender and sex, this model applies equally to gender roles and sexual relations. Implicit in the logic of complementarity is both a biological and cultural reality, and for John Paul II, it is an ontological reality as well. While many of the normative Catholic teachings on marriage and reproduction embed attitudes about gender, certain feminized images and models of the Church obscure such attitudes.

METAPHORS, RHETORIC, AND GENDER

Words and images are powerful, and in official Catholic writings about sex, their power serves a rhetorical purpose. Margaret Melady notes that the aim of rhetorical imagery is "to move auditors to agreement." Metaphoric images move "meaning from the literal to a range of relational possibilities" (Melady 1999, 139). Since metaphors relate one thing in terms of another, they also tend "to narrow vision and reduce options" (139).[16] Metaphors both open up possibilities and reduce them. They free us to think about a thing differently while always directing us to think about it in particular ways. Exploring the meaning and significance of metaphors is an inherently slippery activity. Because imagery is in constant motion (both in the sense of opening up and closing in on itself), we can never pin it down and dissect it; metaphors are dynamic and alive. This does not mean, however, that we cannot capture them, at least briefly, and try to reflect on their effects.

Two very different scholars, one a religious ethicist and one a historian, provide examples of how to capture and evaluate imagery in religious writings. Both offer insights about metaphor and imagery that help focus our discussion about the use of feminine metaphors for the Church. In an interesting analysis of *Humanae Vitae,* Richard Miller, a religious ethicist, suggests that the encyclical has maintained its "enduring appeal" in recent decades because of its "subtext about the proper way to understand women in relation to cultural freedom" (Miller 1996, 152). Miller identifies deep patriarchal biases throughout this document that can only be read through a gender-based critique that is "designed to trace the covert desires nestled beneath the surface of the encyclical's text" (152). Even though there is no explicit presentation of a gender theory in the document—indeed, Miller says that the language of gender is "repressed" in the encyclical—he claims that Paul VI uses allegory to depict an ideology of gender roles.

Miller's attack on *Humanae Vitae* differs from most criticism of the document, because instead of focusing on the explicit moral argumentation, he "unearths" another layer of meaning—and in his view, it is this layer that plays into the overt misogyny of Catholic conservatives (148). Miller draws our attention to two claims the encyclical advances: that "nature" is a physical process, independent of human volition, and that a contraceptive culture is dangerous to the morality of our society. He then illustrates how these two claims are "troped by the language of gender, cast in patriarchal terms" (141). In other words, a particular view of gender results when the term "nature" serves as a trope for woman's body. The encyclical's structuralism, which draws a polar distinction between the male and female, is also allegorical because the binary male/female points to something else, "namely, immanence and transcendence, or nature and culture" (143). Miller concludes that this subtext robs women of agency and makes them subordinate while reinforcing the male's power to "instrumentalize, to structure matter according to some nonmaterial principles, to exert dominion by using raw stuff for opportunistic enjoyment" (143). Miller makes a convincing case for reading papal texts in a way that unearths layers that are often hidden by the explicit moral argumentation. While he extends his analysis beyond metaphorical language to allegory more generally, Miller's study is congruent with my concerns about the gendered metaphors in magisterial documents.

Whereas Miller finds it possible and desirable to read for clues about gender beneath the text, Caroline Walker Bynum is much more cautious in her study of the theme of God and Jesus as mother, at least about gender. Bynum, a historian, resists the claim that attributing maternity to God, even if only metaphorically, tells us anything about gender. She shows the prevalence of this theme in medieval devotional literature, citing in particular Bernard of Clairvaux, Anselm of Canterbury, William of St. Thierry, and Aelred of Rivaulx. Most of these figures were Cistercian monks, a point important to Bynum's study. She situates their use of maternal imagery in the context of "a Cistercian ambivalence about authority and a Cistercian conception of community" (Bynum 1982, 113). She concludes that the metaphors the authors of twelfth-century spiritual writings used do not necessarily reveal what they thought about women and mothers. Rather, they display a crisis in authority and the ambiguity toward it experienced by the authors. Bynum rejects the notion that these feminine metaphors reveal much about gender, but she does think they illuminate matters of authority and community. While Miller is confident that we can unearth a critical view of gender in documents even when they repress the language of gender, Bynum is cautious about reading too much into gendered metaphors. Miller's and Bynum's approaches to interpreting gender affirm that attitudes about gender and about gender roles are intimately connected to structures of authority.

The Church Is Like . . .

It is not unusual to see authors use metaphors and models to describe the Church, in particular to describe its relationship to the laity.[17] Before beginning our exploration into the explicitly gendered metaphors, it is useful to look at the wide range of such metaphors. *Lumen Gentium,* the Dogmatic Constitution of the Church promulgated at the Second Vatican Council, presents a sampling of these, claiming: "Since the Church is a mystery, it cannot be exhaustively defined, but its nature is best communicated by studying the various biblical metaphors" (Abbott 1966, 18). The document identifies four metaphors from the Old Testament: Church as sheepfold, Church as a tract of land (specifically a vineyard), Church as edifice, and Church as mother. The bishops of Vatican II indicate that these images are drawn from everyday facets of life, suggesting that they were intended to personalize the Church.

Each of these metaphors elicits a different sense of what it means to be a Church.[18] The image of a building, for instance, evokes a sense of strength and permanence. Unlike the other metaphors, the image of architecture implies something visible in the world and suggests human participation and effort in the making of the Church. Nevertheless, as a nonhuman metaphor, it suggests an impersonal structure. The image of the sheepfold depicts humans as followers, a marked difference from the powerful image of the Church as building. Christ as the shepherd leading his flock conveys a pastoral, gentle image, but equating the laity with sheep underplays human agency and autonomy. The metaphor of Church as a vineyard emphasizes the nurturing and life-giving aspects of the Church, and in that sense correlates to the maternal metaphors. It also captures the nature of the Church as a place of toil.

The most interesting metaphor for our purposes is the Church as mother.[19] Notably, while the metaphor specifically uses the term "mother," the description blends the image of mother with the image of wife. In fact, the short summary of this metaphor in *Lumen Gentium* appears to emphasize only the spousal aspect of the Church, not the maternal. As the spouse of Christ, "an unbreakable covenant" unites the Church to him. Furthermore, Christ chooses the Church, nourishes her, and expects her to be "subject to Him in love and fidelity" (19). This most personal metaphor places the laity in a very different relationship to Christ. It is at once intensely physical and mystical. The conflation of mother and spouse in this description suggests that the feminine relationship to the male is always defined in physical terms. Both mother and spouse, according to this view, are in service to the male body. Without indicating a preference for one of these biblical metaphors over the others, *Lumen Gentium* proposes two other analogies—ones that the participants of the Second Vatican Council embraced.

The first is the image of Church as the body of Christ: "As all the members of the human body, though they are many, form one body, so also are the faithful in Christ" (Abbott 1966, 20). This thoroughly physical image reinforces the Church's sacramental role. Avery Dulles describes this image as "organic, rather than sociological. It has an inbuilt vital principle thanks to which it can grow, repair itself, and adapt itself to changing needs" (Dulles 1974, 46). The Church is the body, and Christ is the head. Hence, the body is under the control of the head—the head unites, vivifies, and moves the body. The domination of head over body emphasizes the hierarchical relationship of the various parts of the Church.

The body-of-Christ metaphor is clearly connected to the maternal/ spousal one discussed earlier: "Having become the model of a man loving his wife as his own body, Christ loves the Church as His bride. For her part, the Church is subject to her head" (Abbott 1966, 21). This passage is explicit in its affirmation of the femininity of the Church and the connection between the Church as body, mother, and spouse. Yet the confluence of these metaphors defies strict gender distinctions. The Church is the body of Christ (and in that sense it is male), yet it is also like his wife and his mother (and in that sense it is female). It is worth noting, however, that both spousal and body-of-Christ metaphors attempt to capture the sense of the church as a mystical communion. But in both cases, the mystery is described in organic terms: the body and the sexual act in marriage.

The final metaphor, and the one most commonly associated with the changes brought about by the Second Vatican Council, is the Church as people of God. Like the others, this one has a biblical provenance: "a chosen race, a royal priesthood, a holy nation, a purchased people. . . . You who in times past were not a people, but are now the people of God" (1 Peter 2:9–10). According to Dulles's commentary, this image "met a profound desire of the Council to put greater emphasis on the human and communal side of the Church, rather than on the institutional and hierarchical aspects which have sometimes been overstressed in the past for polemical reasons" (Abbott 1966, 24). Unlike the metaphors of body, nature, or architecture, this one captures the sense of an institution as an amalgam of individuals who are connected to God through the act of having been chosen by him. The Church is the people of God. The image of people of God does not differentiate between humans on the basis of race, gender, or ethnicity; it is profoundly egalitarian and democratic.[20]

Lumen Gentium's discussion of the metaphors and images of the Church reveals how pervasive and important this practice is in Catholic ecclesiological discourse. We can gain even more insight by narrowing our focus to the metaphors with explicit gendered connotations, such as the Church as the bride of Christ, the Church as Mary, and the Church as mother.

We noted above the blending of spousal and maternal metaphors, a practice that the use of the Virgin Mary as a metaphor reinforces. Many Catholic documents use the metaphor of Church as spouse to emphasize the indissolubility of the marital bond. An early and interesting example is from an address by Pope Pius XII that conveys the sacramentality of marriage through the analogy of widows to the Church and the deceased spouse to Christ. He proclaims the "greatness of widowhood" and compares it to "the Church Militant" who is "deprived of visions of its heavenly spouse, but still unfailingly united to him" (Liebard 1978, 194). In this context, the deceased husband is similar to "Christ who delivers Himself to save mankind," while the widow is like "the redeemed Church which accepts its part in the sacrifice of Christ" (194). The implication here is that by dying, the husband becomes even more Christlike, and that by accepting her suffering, the widow becomes more like the Church.

This passage highlights the image of the Church as passive sufferer and correlates the emphasis on suffering with gender by equating the body-of-Christ metaphor with female suffering. A more recent example of the connection between suffering and gender is from the 1994 version of the catechism which places the metaphor of the Church as body of Christ in the context of the Eucharist: "The Church which is the Body of Christ participates in the offering of her Head" (United States Catholic Conference 1914, 1368). While this suggests a clear dichotomy between the head and the body, the two are united because "in the Eucharist the sacrifice of Christ becomes also the sacrifice of the members of his Body" (1368). The body of Christ is clearly feminine in this model: "[T]he Church is often represented as a woman in prayer, arms outstretched in the praying position. Like Christ who stretched out his arms on the cross, through him, with him, and in him, she offers herself and intercedes for all men" (United States Catholic Conference 1994, 1368).

In *Lumen Gentium,* Christian spouses are said to "partake of the mystery of that unity and fruitful love which exists between Christ and His Church" (Abbott 1966, 28–29). The correlation between the Christ/church relationship and the marital covenant has a long history. In fact, it seems plausible that the Old Testament metaphor of God as

GENDER

113

a faithful God and Israel as an unfaithful harlot influenced Catholic imagery. Theologian Francis Schüssler Fiorenza notes a problem with such imagery: if in fact the equation of Christ and the Church with the marriage relationship is linked to the prophetic tradition's description of a contrast between a faithful God and an unfaithful harlot, then that might lead to the unintentional association of "the husband with a faithful God and the wife with a fickle harlot." Fiorenza continues, "It also makes the husband superior to the wife and places her along with children and slaves in a subordinate obediential position" (Fiorenza 2001, 325). Fiorenza's concern that the imagery is not innocuous because it can affect human relationships is pertinent to all of these gendered metaphors. The fact that the metaphors for the Church are predominantly feminine is not a coincidence: it supports Catholic attitudes about gender.

In *Mulieres Dignitatem,* Pope John Paul II addresses the gender implications of the spousal metaphor. He begins by describing the biblical passages that support this analogy. In addition to the Letter to the Ephesians, he also turns to the prophet Isaiah to show that this analogy "transfers to the New Testament what was already contained *in the Old Testament*" (John Paul II 1988, par. 23). He acknowledges that the comparison of intrahuman relationships with God-human relationships has limitations: "[W]e must *distinguish* that element which expresses the human reality of interpersonal relations from that which expresses in symbolic language the 'great mystery' which is divine" (par. 23). Nevertheless, the human institution of marriage "explains" the union of Christ and the Church, and the union of Christ and the Church transforms the union of man and woman into a sacrament. He acknowledges that the human reality influences and is influenced by the symbolic language.

John Paul II responds more directly to the sort of criticism that theologians such as Fiorenza level about the hierarchical nature of the spousal metaphor by addressing the controversial passage from the Letter to the Ephesians where women are told to be subject to their husbands.[21] He believes that the true meaning of this passage is that wives and husbands are to subject themselves to each other mutually; he argues that the true meaning of subjection is to give oneself up to the other. Thus, since Christ, as the head of the Church, gave himself up, the husband, like Christ, must sacrifice himself. In the case of human spouses, the subjection must be mutual, whereas in the marriage between Christ and Church, only the Church is subject (par. 24).

In these examples, we see the confluence of various metaphors—church as mother, church as bride, and church as widow. All three of these images describe relations of women to men, and all three capture experiences that are familiar to most persons. Nevertheless, not all women experience these roles, nor do any men. The spousal metaphor captures the submissive aspect of the feminine, especially when combined with the body-of-Christ imagery. The maternal metaphor that we have already mentioned takes on several different forms and it often overlaps with the spousal metaphor. In Catholicism, the most exemplary model, especially for women, is Mary. Her ideal qualities must also be emulated by the Church. We look in the next section at the maternal metaphor exemplified in the figure of Mary.

. . . Mary—Virgin and Mother

What does it mean to say that the Church ought to model itself on Mary? John Paul II offers a detailed exposition of Mary and her significance for understanding the nature of the Church in his 1987 encyclical letter *Redemptoris Mater*. In the letter, he distinguishes between the fleshly and the spiritual dimensions of motherhood and claims that Mary embodies the link between these two dimensions. By being at the center of both "the moment of the Incarnation of the Word" and the birth of the Church, Mary became the exemplary model. She participated in the physical action of giving birth to Christ, and the spiritual action of her powerful faith and obedience gave birth, as it were, to the Church. This dual participation is acknowledged in the New Testament account of Mary's encounter with Elizabeth: Elizabeth calls Mary blessed twice, first for the fruit of her womb and second for her faith.

The discussion of the passage in the Gospel of Luke where a woman says to Jesus "blessed is the womb that bore you and the breasts you have sucked" (Luke 11:27) reinforces this dualism between Mary's physical and spiritual participation in the theological drama of the incarnation. Jesus responds, "Blessed rather are those who hear the word of God and keep it" (Luke 11:28). John Paul II interprets this passage as Jesus' attempt "to divert attention from motherhood," understood as a fleshly bond, and to direct it toward the mysterious bond of the spirit (John Paul II 1987, par. 20). The diversion from motherhood has a theological purpose. The emphasis on Mary's physical maternity draws attention to Jesus' physicality—to the fleshly bond between mother and son. Jesus' response to the woman reminds believers that the more important bond between this mother and son comes from her faith—from hearing and keeping God's word. For the pope, the diversion of attention from Mary's womb and breasts does not mean that Jesus was rejecting her role in giving birth to him. Instead, he thinks that her more significant contribution was her faith: "[A]lready at the Annunciation she accepted the word of God, because she believed it, *because she was obedient to God,* and because she 'kept' the word and 'pondered it in her heart' and by means of her whole life accomplished it" (par. 20).

Like Mary, then, the Church "becomes herself a mother. . . . From Mary the Church also learns her own motherhood" (par. 43). She becomes obedient and faithful. John Paul II elucidates this analogy in a different way—one that emphasizes the generative aspect of maternity. He writes, "If the Church is the sign and instrument of intimate union with God, she is so by reason of her motherhood, because, receiving life from the Spirit, she 'generates' sons and daughters of the human race to a new life in Christ" (43). This act of generation reflects the new spiritual motherhood that Jesus was encouraging in the passage from Luke.

Although the Church is a mother in the general sense, Mary's distinctive and unique motherhood is the model for human maternal qualities. The relevant aspect of Mary's maternity, the one that distinguishes it, according to these documents, is her faith. The encyclical letter describes Mary as "the first to believe." In fact, the pope contrasts her with to the first woman to sin, Eve. Eve had little faith and was disobedient; Mary had boundless faith. Quoting from St. Irenaeus, the pope states: "The knot of Eve's disobedience was untied by Mary's obedience; what the virgin Eve bound through her unbelief, the Virgin Mary *loosened by her faith*" (par. 19).[22] Her consent at the annunciation was evidence of her faith, as was her desire to always remain true to God. It is noteworthy that in this context Mary's virginity is less about sexuality and more about fidelity. Even the contrast between

Mary and Eve, which is often drawn as a contrast between sexuality and virginity, is seen as symbolic of fidelity. According to the encyclical, when Mary uttered the phrase "Behold, I am the handmaid of the Lord," she pledged herself both to motherhood and virginity (par. 39). Virginity, then, is a sign and attitude of ultimate fidelity and total self-giving; it describes her relationship to God.[23]

A careful reading of both *Lumen Gentium* and *Redemptoris Mater* reveals two distinct descriptions of the relationship between Church, Mary, and motherhood. Mary's motherhood is not just a model for the Church to emulate, it describes a reality that the Church has already achieved. The Church, like Mary, *is* indeed a virgin and a mother. Mary exemplifies to the Church what that virginity and maternity entail. For example, in *Lumen Gentium,* the bishops of Vatican II write "the Church herself is a virgin, who keeps whole and pure the fidelity she has pledged to her Spouse. Imitating the Mother of her Lord, and by the power of the Holy Spirit, she preserves with virginal purity and integral faith, a firm hope, and a sincere charity" (Abbott 1966, 93). John Paul II quotes this very passage from Vatican II and supplements it with the observation that we know that the Church is the spouse of Christ "from the Pauline Letters (cf. Eph. 5: 21–33; 2 Cor. 11:2) and from the title found in John: 'bride of the Lamb' (Rev. 21:9)" (John Paul II 1987, par. 43). Hence, to say that Mary (or motherhood, or virginity) serves simply as a cultural metaphor or analogy seems to miss much of what this "ecclesial Mariology" is about. The Catholic tradition believes that the Church is a mother and a virgin.

What is the significance of this confluence of imagery to the study of gender, order, and authority in Catholic sexual ethics? The most obvious response to that question lies in the feminine expression of this imagery. Mary is a model not only for the Church but especially for women because, as John Paul II writes, "femininity has a unique relationship with the Mother of the Redeemer" (par. 46). Consequently, she has a special relevance to women; it is from her that they can learn more about womanhood. Many have noted that the Marian ideals of virginity and maternity are mutually exclusive for most women. Nevertheless, according to the encyclical, Mary reveals the "secrets of living their femininity with dignity" (par. 46). It is interesting that while Catholicism depicts womanhood as an essential and natural concept (that is, rather than as a cultural construction), women need assistance to learn its performance. Mary's life is a witness to "feminine qualities" to which all women must aspire. These are: "self-offering totality of love," the capacity for "bearing the greatest sorrows," "limitless fidelity," "tireless devotion to work," and the "ability to combine penetrating intuition with words of support and encouragement" (46). That Mary is a role model for the Church and for women would seem to suggest that the Church is feminine in her qualities. Hence, it is noteworthy that these "feminine" qualities reflect passivity rather than great power or authority. They do, however, capture certain aspects of the Church's role in the world.

... an Adopting Mother

Other passages in the magisterial literature rely on the language of adoption to describe the maternal aspect of the Church. The image of adopting mother is perhaps a more realistic description of the Church's role. Yet its emphasis on the femininity of the Church is notable—the Church is not an adopting father. In *Redemptoris Mater,* the comparison of the Church to Mary emphasizes the role of adopting mother: "For, just as *Mary is at the service of the mystery of the Incarnation, so the Church* is always *at the service of the mystery of adoption to sonship* through grace" (John Paul II 1987, par. 43).

Pius XI's *Casti Connubii* also uses the metaphor of adopting mother. While discussing the birth of children as "amongst the blessings of marriage" the pope emphasizes that the role of parents is not to "transmit sanctification to their progeny" but rather to "offer their offspring to the Church" (Pius XI 1930, 9). When parents present their children to the Church for baptism, the Church becomes their mother. She sanctifies them by erasing, as it were, the original sin which by "the very process of generating life has become the way of death" (9). Thus, one inherits original sin through physical birth and becomes a "partaker of immortal life" through spiritual rebirth (9). In this instance, the maternal metaphor embodies remarkable powers. Moreover, Pius XI contrasts the maternal Church, who "regenerates through the laver of Baptism unto supernatural justice," with the human mother, who passes original sin to her progeny. In the next paragraph, the pope addresses Christian mothers directly. He assures each mother that joy will overwhelm the pains of childbirth and the cares of childrearing: "she will rejoice in the Lord crowned as it were with the glory of her offspring" (10). This passage is interesting because it appears to diminish the important work of childbirth and childrearing. Nevertheless, by describing the Church as an adopting mother, the metaphor seems to value some aspects of maternity.

... a Mother

Many of the Catholic documents associate the maternal metaphor with the Marian metaphor, though this is not always the case. Sometimes the Church is a mother without reference to Mary. A notable instance from the early 1960s is John XXIII's encyclical letter *Mater et Magistra*.[24] The importance of the Church as mother is clear from the title (mother and teacher), and the pope uses this metaphor to frame his discussion of Catholic social teaching. He begins by stating that Jesus established the Church as mother and teacher and entrusted her with "the double task of begetting sons unto herself, and of educating and governing those whom she begets, guiding with maternal providence the life both of individuals and of peoples" (O'Brien and Shannon 1992, 84). Begetting, as we have seen, is the task most associated with women in the documents on marriage. Educating offspring is associated with parenting in general, so it has both masculine and feminine aspects. Governing is, by contrast, a more public act—one traditionally reserved for the male members of society. Of course, the Church that governs is male, but this brief description of its femininity in the context of power is noteworthy. In the title, the distinction drawn between mother and teacher coincides, at least partially, with the complementarity model. So, like the human, who in the state of "original solitude" is both male and female, the Church encompasses both elements.

Pope John XXIII specifies the maternal nature of the Church's task. His language in the introduction suggests that the feminine aspect is connected with the responsibility of being "solicitous for the requirements of men in their daily lives, not merely those relating to food and sustenance, but also to their comfort and advancement in various kinds of goods and in varying circumstances of time" (84). The mention of providing food reinforces the image of maternal nurture, as

GENDER

119

does the role of comforting. In both these descriptions, one can see the effect of expectations related to gender roles. The most direct expression of this appears when the pope notes that the life and ministry of Jesus consisted of both the authoritarian role of teaching and commanding his followers and the compassionate role of concern for "the earthly needs of mankind" (84).

The mother/teacher metaphor for the Church continues in the present with the papacy of John Paul II. In his apostolic exhortation on the role of the family (*Familiaris Consortio*), he distinguishes the two roles of the Church but then insists that "it is one and the same Church that is both Teacher and Mother" (John Paul II 1981, par. 33). In its teaching role, the Church "interprets the moral norm and proposes it to all people of good will, without concealing its demands of radicalness and perfection" (par. 33); as mother, it is attuned to the difficulties faced by married couples. The important point is that the empathy and compassion that emerges from the Church's maternal aspect must never lead it astray from the task of upholding the truth: "The Church must always remain linked with her doctrine and never separated from it" (par. 33). This link between the Church's maternal nurture and the enforcement of moral doctrine provides an example of the use of feminine language in a broader context that extends beyond marriage and reproduction to moral theology more generally. It is this link that is most suggestive of the connection between gender, authority, and moral order.

MORAL THEOLOGY AND THE FEMININE CHURCH

In the encyclical letters *Veritatis Splendor* (1993) and *Evangelium Vitae* (1995), Pope John Paul II uses maternal images to convey a series of messages about moral theology. The earlier encyclical addresses questions of moral theology related to the sources of morality and to method in moral reasoning. More specifically, he frames the letter as a response to moral theologians who are challenging absolutism in Catholic moral theology by encouraging some flexibility in the application of moral norms to particular situations. In the letter, John Paul II warns the faithful to avoid theories such as proportionalism, consequentialism, and relativism. *Evangelium Vitae,* a less-theoretical document, focuses almost entirely on the exceptionless moral prohibitions against the direct killing of innocent persons. It develops the broader theoretical concerns of *Veritatis Splendor* in the context of specific moral problems, such as euthanasia, abortion, the death penalty, contraception, and assisted reproduction. Both documents warn the faithful of great dangers in the world and urge them to submit to church teaching. John Paul II uses these encyclicals to exert the Church's authority over the interpretation and teaching of moral norms.

Veritatis Splendor and *Evangelium Vitae* both employ the metaphor of the Church as mother to soften the harshness of their absolutist approach. As in John XXIII's social encyclical, *Mater et Magistra,* John Paul II's encyclicals describe the Church as having two roles: mother and teacher. The pope distinguishes these roles from each other as two aspects of the same unity. To a certain extent, mother and teacher mirror the relationship of complementarity between man and woman—each has a particular role but is always dependent on the other. These two roles are not, however, gendered male and female. The pope describes them both as female, which is ironic since the actual teaching voice of the magisterium is in reality always male (popes, bishops, etc.).

In both *Evangelium Vitae* and *Veritatis Splendor,* the Virgin Mary is the ultimate model for the moral life: "Mary is the radiant sign and inviting model of the moral life" (John Paul II 1993, par.120). She combines merciful compassion and empathy for all sinners with a determination to protect moral law from "beguiling doctrines, even in the areas of philosophy and theology" (par. 120).

Veritatis Splendor invokes the maternal metaphor to describe the Church as compassionate and understanding. The Church as teacher interprets and defends "the universal and permanent validity of the precepts prohibiting intrinsically evil acts" (par. 95); as mother, the Church expresses compassion about the difficulty of upholding absolute norms. John Paul II presents the Church's maternal compassion as a contrast to its perceived "intransigence" about the permanence and immutability of certain moral norms. He writes, "The Church, one hears, is lacking in understanding and compassion. But the Church's motherhood [here he means its compassion and understanding] can never in fact be separated from her teaching mission" (par. 95).[25] Despite this acknowledgement of the Church's compassionate side, throughout the encyclical the Church functions as the tough-minded teacher who interprets, proclaims, and defends absolute norms. The encyclical describes the pedagogical role as a duty that emerges from the Church's status as "the faithful Bride of Christ." Even the role of teacher is gendered as female. Nevertheless, the Church's role as mother is central and cannot be separated from its teaching role. The Church expresses simultaneously its motherhood and its teaching mission when it stands fast in protecting the moral truth. The pope writes that "genuine understanding and compassion must mean love for the person, for his [sic] true good, for his [sic] authentic freedom. And this does not result, certainly, from concealing or weakening moral truth, but rather from proposing it in its most profound meaning as an outpouring of God's eternal wisdom" (par. 95).

Evangelium Vitae uses the term "mother" to refer to the Church, to nature, to Mary, or to women in general. To a certain extent, these various uses all converge to mean the same thing. The image of the Church as mother appears in the final chapter, which begins with a meditation on the mystery of the birth of Christ and on Mary's consent to carry the child. John Paul II connects Mary and the Church because they are both "a mother of all who are reborn to life" (John Paul II 1995, par. 102). Moreover, the Church's relationship to Mary as mother is dialectical. The Church discovers "the meaning of her own motherhood and the way in which she is called to express it" by contemplating Mary, while at the same time, "the Church's experience of motherhood leads to a most profound understanding of Mary's experience as the *incomparable model of how life should be welcomed and cared for*" (par. 102).

The encyclical compares the Church's "constant tension with the forces of evil which still roam the world and affect human hearts" as "pangs and 'the labor of childbirth,' " a metaphor that makes the Church as mother even more realistic and physical.[26] Thus, the Church, like Mary before her, has "had to live her motherhood amid suffering" (par. 102). In these passages, motherhood is not merely nurture, education and compassion; it is also the physical labor of childbirth. It is interesting that the pain of that physical labor describes the Church's struggle with evil.

The fact that abortion is a prominent issue in this text might offer one explanation for the many references to motherhood in *Evangelium*

Vitae, especially the reference to labor and childbirth. This encyclical is a definitive statement of the Catholic opposition to abortion, which includes opposition to all cases, even when the mother's life or well-being is at risk. The pope acknowledges the tremendous cost of this prohibition to Catholic women. Indeed, he commends the heroic, silent witness of brave mothers "who devote themselves to their own family without reserve, who suffer in giving birth to children and who are ready to make any effort, to face any sacrifice, in order to pass on to them the best of themselves" (par. 86). He is also concerned about the pervasiveness of cultural models that discourage motherhood. He blames the media for promoting a view that diminishes the values of fidelity, chastity, and sacrifice and that describes these values as obsolete for "Christian wives and mothers." The pope's valorization of this suffering is evident in his praise of mothers: "We thank you, heroic mothers, for your invincible love: We thank you for your intrepid trust in God and in his love. We thank you for the sacrifice of your life" (par. 86).

These two important encyclicals use the trope of the Church as maternal figure both to say something about the Church and to make a statement about the role of women. In both cases, the feminine metaphor stands in for an aspect of church authority—its role in imposing order in a world that threatens Catholic morality and its "gospel of life." This sense of order as discipline is especially relevant to the area of moral theology where there has been a significant debate recently about the scope of the Church's authority over morality. One question at the heart of the debate is Can the Church proclaim a moral norm to be absolute—that is, without exception? While the maternal metaphor in *Veritatis Splendor* supports the argument that there are absolute moral norms, it also tries to moderate the harshness of such norms by acknowledging the Church's compassion and understanding. One should not, however, interpret the Church's compassion as a lack of firmness; the universal and unchanging moral norms require Catholics to display a "heroic commitment" (John Paul II 1993, par. 94). Martyrdom, the ultimate example of such a commitment, is "an affirmation of the inviolability of God's moral order" (par. 92). Christians must be ready to suffer and sacrifice to ward off "a headlong plunge into the most dangerous crisis which can afflict man: the *confusion between good and evil*" (par. 93). In the end, the Church must wage battle and the faithful must be willing to bear the costs of that battle. While mother Church is unbending and disciplined in her proclamations about good and evil, *Veritatis Splendor* gives believers some comfort in the faith that Mary "understands sinful man and loves him with a mother's joy" (par. 120).

COLLECTIVE GUILT AND THE MATERNAL METAPHOR

We can also find evidence of the pervasiveness of the maternal metaphor in recent Vatican documents on reconciliation in the context of the celebration of the new millennium. Two documents in particular, *Tertio Millennio Adveniente,* the pope's 1994 apostolic letter on preparations for the Great Jubilee of the Year 2000, and *Memory and Reconciliation: The Church and the Faults of the Past,* a document prepared by the Vatican's International Theological Commission in 1999, contain numerous examples of maternal metaphors.

The 2000 Jubilee was significant for Pope John Paul II. He admitted, "In fact, preparing for the *Year 2000 has become as it were a hermeneutical key to my pontificate*" (John Paul II 1994, par. 23). A central feature of these preparations was the pope's call for penance and reconciliation. The apostolic letter notes that the many disturbing experiences of the twentieth century demonstrate "that the world needs purification; it needs to be converted" (par. 18). The Church is to play a role in this purification by becoming "more conscious of the sinfulness of her children" and acknowledging "as her own her sinful sons and daughters" (par. 33). This way of framing the issue passes any blame that the Church as an institutional entity bears, especially any responsibility it may have had for the Holocaust of the Jewish people, to the laity.[27] The metaphor imputes guilt to the children (the laity), while the mother (Church) bears their sorrows. This metaphorical way to talk about the Church obfuscates the true meaning of the Church. It emphasizes the tension that *Lumen Gentium* describes between viewing the Church as a human institution and viewing it as "a sacrament of intimate union with God" (Abbott 1966, 15).

The International Theological Commission document also uses maternal metaphors. The authors devote a subsection to "The Motherhood of the Church" under the section entitled "Theological Foundations." They begin by acknowledging the long heritage of the idea

"Mater Ecclesia" (Mother Church) in Christian theology, noting Augustine, Cyprian of Carthage, and Paulinus of Nola. They use this image for a specific purpose, as a way to distinguish between the sins of the faithful and the purity of the Church. The Church, in the commission's view, "confesses herself a sinner, but not as a subject who sins, but rather in assuming the weight of her children's faults in maternal solidarity, so as to cooperate in overcoming them through penance and newness of life" (International Theological Commission 1998, par. 3.4).

The authors, however, emphasize that this distinction is not always clear. They write that "each baptized person can be considered to be at the same time a child of the Church, in that he [sic] is generated in her to divine life, and Mother Church, in that, by his faith and love he cooperates in giving birth to new children for God" (3.4). This interesting passage suggests that the believer is an individual component of the larger Church, but also to some extent each believer embodies the whole Church. The document delineates the dual roles the believer plays—as child of the Church and as the Church itself. The authors claim that the believer "is ever more Mother Church, the greater is his [sic] holiness and the more ardent is his effort to communicate to others the gift he has received" (3.4). Yet "the baptized person does not cease to be a child of the Church when, because of sin, he [sic] separates himself from her in his heart" (3.4).

Both the pope and the International Theological Commission utilize the maternal image of the Church bearing the sins of her children to illustrate the sense of responsibility that the Church feels for its actions. It is, however, a metaphor open to various interpretations. As we have seen, describing the Church as a mother is certainly not a new phenomenon—it can be traced back to the early Church fathers.[28] A more recent document, Vatican II's *Lumen Gentium,* describes the Church as "becoming herself a mother" as a result of contemplation on Mary's mysterious sanctity. *Lumen* also employs the other characteristic of Mary—her virginity—to emphasize the Church's purity and fidelity (Abbott 1966, 93).

The reference to virginity is interesting in this context and perhaps provides an important clue about the significance of the pure and unblemished status of the Church. Joseph Plumpe remarks that the description of the Church as virgin may have preceded the identification of Church as mother. The personification of the Church as a virgin implies "that she was ever solicitous to protect her body, the faithful everywhere, against contamination and harm through erroneous doctrine" (Plumpe, 28). The Church must defend its virginity against false doctrine and heresy.

To many, particularly those outside the Church, reliance on this imagery in the context of repentance for actions toward the Jewish people seems to obscure the repentance itself. In one reading of the metaphor, it reveals the failure of the Church to take adequate responsibility for its actions. This suggests that the metaphor's central purpose is to explain how the Church can ask forgiveness for actions while maintaining holiness. It establishes a distance between the Church and the laity (her sinful children) that keeps the Church secure in holiness while placing the burden of the sins on the laity. As Francis Sullivan notes, while the distinction between Church as mother and her children as sinners solves the problem of how to reconcile the Church's holiness with the request for forgiveness, it does leave two negative consequences. First, it overlooks the fact that some of the children were in fact members of the hierarchy of the Church. Second, it hides the fact that some of the policies and practices of the Church "have been objectively in contradiction to the Gospel and have caused harm to many people" (Sullivan 2000, 18). For Sullivan, this metaphor muddies the issue of responsibility.[29]

One way to make better sense of this metaphor is to see it in the context of the familial imagery in *Tertio Millennio*. For example, in the first paragraph of the letter, the pope introduces the coming of the third millennium by reminding the faithful that God sent forth his son, born of woman, so that all "might receive adoption as sons and daughters" (John Paul II 1994, par.1). One could argue that such imagery is inevitable since the pope is describing an event that celebrates Christ's birth. In fact, John Paul II places the Jubilee year in the context of the Marian year (1986/1987) and the Year of the Family (1994), both of which the pope claims anticipate the Jubilee.

Viewed in this context, the metaphor of Church as mother seems less rhetorical. In this more positive light, the maternal image evokes a sense of closeness between a mother and her children as she comforts them and bears their burdens. Even when we contextualize the metaphor, it is difficult to miss the gender aspect of the metaphor: the

Church is a mother, not a father. These documents on reconciliation make no mention of the implications of connecting the Church, a male-dominated hierarchy, with motherhood, a role associated with women. This particular image of the Church's maternity focuses on its role as consoler and bearer of burdens—a role distinct from the image of Church as teacher. John Paul II writes in *Veritatis Splendor* that the Church in her maternal role exhibits "genuine understanding and compassion" about the often difficult demands of the moral life, while the Church as teacher "never tires of proclaiming the moral norm" (John Paul II 1993, 117).[30] These various aspects of the Church's maternity all focus on the same goal: maintaining the order of God's creation.

GENDER, METAPHORS, AND AUTHORITY

Official descriptions of the Church as a mother in the contexts of moral theology and the theology of reconciliation reinforce the strict gender-role assignment associated with the model of complementarity. They also suggest interesting implications in the areas of ecclesiology and church governance. The Church, when understood as an institution, represents power and authority over matters related to practice and dogma. Recent debates about the Church's authority to teach definitively take on a different texture when we view them through the lens of these metaphors. For example, we have noted already that in recent history, some Catholic theologians have vigorously contested the status and changeable nature of these teachings on sex and reproduction. To claim that the Church has revised its teaching appears to some to contradict the belief that the Church is competent to teach truthfully and absolutely. The debate about regulating reproduction is just as much a debate about what it means for the Church to teach with authority. Or, put more broadly, it is about what it means to be a living tradition. A sense of nostalgia for the past is implicit in these metaphors, which some might interpret as a longing for the maternal. In his strong criticisms of the papacy, Gary Wills finds the centrality of the Virgin Mary in the lives of celibate priests revealing. He notes that a study commissioned by American bishops found that strong attachment and devotion to the Virgin Mary affected the formation of priests' attitudes toward consecrated virginity. The study, which was canceled before being released, found "mother dominance, or a presence of a dominant unconscious mother image" in the priests (Wills 2000, 204).

In chapter 2, I illustrated how chastity, understood in the context of the theology of marriage, represents an attitude of obedience. The sacrament of marriage, in expressing the marriage of Christ and the Church, signifies different levels of obedience—of bodily desire to the will, of the individual to the Church, of the female to the male, of the body to nature, and ultimately of the Church to Christ. In the context of calling the Church female, obedience and femininity coincide to ensure moral order in the realm of sexual ethics. Yet the logical dissonance that appears when the Church excludes women from participating the priesthood is a sign of disorder. In other words, the governing institutions of the Church are male, yet it evokes its feminine side for rhetorical purposes.

How significant is it that many images for the Church are feminine? This imagery is an essential component of John Paul II's theology of the body. His elucidation of Adam and Eve's creation as the original male and female relies on the symbolism of the Church as the female body of Christ. Eve, like the Church, complements Adam, who, like Christ, is male. This imagery has many implications for sexual morality, most strikingly in the case of homosexuality. If the Church is female and Christ male, then the spousal love between them can only be female to male; male-male or female-female love is not complementary. The Church clearly puts forth other arguments from natural law and scripture to condemn homosexuality, but this theological argument about the body of Christ reveals the potency of the metaphorical language.[31]

In *Mulieres Dignitatem,* John Paul II reflects further on the significance and implications of using feminine metaphors to describe the Church. He acknowledges that these analogies are meant to capture a certain reality, but he also argues that they create a reality. So about the image of the Church as the bride of Christ, for instance, he writes, "According to this conception, *all human beings—both women and men—are called* through the Church, *to be the 'Bride' of Christ, the Redeemer of the world.* In this way 'being the bride,' and thus the 'feminine' element, becomes a symbol of all that is 'human,' according to the words of Paul: 'There is neither male nor female; for you are all *one* in Christ Jesus (Gal 3:28)' " (John Paul II 1988, par. 25). This oneness emerges from John Paul II's reading of the creation story. His interpretation of the "unity of the two" as complementary is another way of saying that for all persons, the primary mode of expressing relationality is through "spousal love"—a love that Christ's love for the Church exemplifies.

These feminine metaphors are necessary, according to the pope, because Catholics would be unable to grasp the mystery of the Church without them. This implies that the feminine enables the faithful to understand the human. In John Paul II's view, "The Bible convinces us of the fact that one can have no adequate hermeneutic of man, or of what is 'human,' without appropriate reference to what is 'feminine.' There is an analogy in God's salvific economy: if we wish to understand it fully in relation to the whole of human history, we cannot omit, in the perspective of our faith, the mystery of 'woman': virgin-mother-spouse" (par. 22).

He also emphasizes that "*the symbol of the Bridegroom is masculine*" (par. 25). In his view, this symbolism has great import for the dignity of women, because Christ was exemplary in his treatment of women. John Paul II claims that Christ "*revealed* the dignity of the 'daughters of Abraham' (cf. Lk 13:16), *the dignity belonging to women* from the very 'beginning' on an equal footing with men" (par. 25). According to the pope, that the Church calls men to be bridegrooms like Christ does not imply that they rule over women. Rather, it is a model for how men ought to treat women.

Another way to pose the question about the significance of this cluster of metaphors is to ask whether and how this metaphor affects either the Church or the category of the feminine. Does it transform them or does it undermine them? I borrow these questions from Lisa Cahill's discussion of another prominent metaphor in official Vatican documents that describes the family as a domestic church. Cahill explores the meaning and implications of this metaphor in historical context. She thinks it is a powerful and useful metaphor, but, like all metaphors, it has the potential to obscure important realities. Cahill states that her study is guided by the question of "[w]hether considering the family as church transforms families or undermines the church" (Cahill 2000, 48).

This concern is significant, because although in recent years there has been an association between "family values" and conservative Christianity, the family's mission can appear to run counter to that of Christianity. As Cahill states, "[F]amilies tend to create solidarity around their own well-being, although the most distinctively Christian moral virtue is sacrifice for the well-being of others." Hence, juxtaposing family and Christianity is inherently problematic. The more immediate issue for Cahill is the effect the metaphor might have on each entity. Describing the family as church risks "making religion subservient to the values and functions of kinship." In other words, its association with family harms the concept "church." Conversely, because "anti-gospel social hierarchies" govern church structures, there is a negative potential to "bringing family religious experience into line with ecclesial hierarchies and limits" (48).

The full significance of the metaphor of family as church depends on what one means by the terms "family" and "church." Both are culturally charged terms capable of nuance and change. These same problems plague the gendered metaphors Vatican authors use to describe the Church. Like the term "family," the term "mother" has various connotations, but it presents a set of unique problems. For example, the metaphorical association can both transform and undermine the terms "mother" and "church." To call the Church mother highlights certain aspects of maternity, and, as we have seen, the magisterial documents often focus on different facets of maternity. In some cases, the mother softens the harsh stance of the Church; in others, she bears the burdens for her children's sins, and so forth.

More interesting for our purposes of identifying the nexus between gender, sex, and authority is to explore the way that calling the Church mother might transform it. As we have noted, finding adequate terms to describe the church is a challenge for Catholicism: "[T]he Church . . . is a mystery that cannot be totally contained by a human concept" (Congregation for the Doctrine of Faith 2000, 18). Yet the human concepts that Vatican documents consistently use are the feminine sexualized roles. On the face of it, one could suggest that the feminine metaphors are a way of ascribing power to women in the Church, but the reality belies that fact. The Church is a hierarchy that consists of males only, and males who are authorized to have a physical relationship with only one woman in their lives—their mother. Thus, what might appear to be a feminization of the Church (calling her by female names) has little effect on the authority of real women.

The danger of these feminine metaphors for the Church is that they tend to subsume and obscure unequal gender roles. A lengthy passage from theologian Paul Quay, who is expounding on the meaning of the bride-of-Christ metaphor, illustrates this tendency:

> *Christ's love was not given to the Church for any merit on her own part. The Father freely chose this people as His Son's bride; and Christ loves her because she is the Father's choice for Him. He had to win her for Himself by His battle with Satan upon the cross. He espoused her there when His side was pierced, His Heart was opened, and water flowed forth, the sign of the bridal bath of baptism. He had not found her worthy of Himself; only His death made her to be a bride without spot or wrinkle or any such thin. Her beauty was His gift alone.*

As a husband with his wife, it is Christ who is the initiator of union with His Church. As God is masculine with respect to the whole of His creation and with respect to the whole of humanity, Christ is masculine with regards to His Church. The Church has no initiative in relation to Christ except that which Christ has already given to her. Without His grace, she can do nothing. (Quay 1985, 56)

This passage illustrates the connection between the symbolic reality the metaphors create and the lived reality of male and female roles. While Quay does not speak for the official Church, his analysis of the spousal metaphor simply takes it to its logical conclusion.

Quay is a leading defender of a conservative Catholic sexual ethic. His analysis of these metaphors reflects a particular agenda. He does, however, offer a helpful analysis of sexual symbolism as it appears in Christian scripture. He notes that in one meaning, sexual symbols take something that is not sexual and use it to symbolize something that is (e.g., snake for male sexual organ). The other type of sexual symbol, and the one more pertinent to this study, is when sexuality or any of its elements (sex organs, sex acts, marriage, childbirth) symbolize "things other than themselves and beyond themselves, of spiritual things that are not sexual at all" (42). For Quay, the theological meaning of this latter type of sexual symbolism is that human sexuality best expresses "the deepest and the highest truths about the relations between God and man," and this fact serves to confirm the goodness of human sexuality (54). So, for example, Christ instituted the sacrament of marriage "to symbolize something far beyond it." Indeed, "God has made marriage to symbolize relationships more intimate than its own sexual relationships, stronger, more tender, more open, more demanding" (55).

The metaphors I have discussed in this section exemplify this second type of sexual symbolism. If one agrees with Quay, then this appropriation of human sexuality points unambiguously to the goodness of human sexuality. Marriage symbolizes the relationship of God to humans. By confirming this proper order of the divine to the human, marriage reflects the goodness of human sexuality. The problem, in my view, is that there is little room in such an interpretation to probe whether this ordering of gender through the institutions of human marriage or the male-only priesthood reflects the principles of justice. Quay's interpretation accepts the metaphors uncritically and ignores any practical effect they might have on lived human sexuality. I offer a different, more critical, reading of these gendered metaphors. In my view, these metaphors appropriate certain human experiences and place them in a larger religious scheme that reinforces a gendered order that has profound implications for Catholic sexual ethics.

Another, and perhaps more positive, interpretation of this feminine imagery might be that describing the Church as woman honors women and reflects a more positive attitude toward motherhood, marriage, and sexuality. Bynum considers and rejects this interpretation when she tries to explain the increased use of maternal and conjugal metaphors in the twelfth century. She argues that while mothers are romanticized and marriage has a certain mystique, the general status of women in the twelfth century showed no improvement. Furthermore, the men who had popularized this feminine imagery were men "who had renounced family and the company of women" (Bynum 1982, 142–44). Bynum bases her conclusion on her belief that the female and the feminine are distinct: "[T]he former is a person of one gender; the latter may be an aspect of a person of either gender" (167). She concludes that one should not take feminine imagery to reveal what the monks in her study thought about actual females.

It might be impossible to know exactly what these metaphors mean. One could try to identify the intentions behind their use or to quantify the exact effect of these metaphors, but even then it would be difficult to arrive at conclusive evidence. Perhaps the best we can do is to note the ambiguity these metaphors pose in the context of Catholic sexual ethics. Unlike gender complementarity, which tells us unambiguously how Catholicism understands gender, these metaphors complicate the order that Catholicism strives to achieve. As far as conclusions about the ultimate effects of this complication, I can only venture that it provides an opening for those eager to see change in Catholic sexual ethics.

5 CONCLUSION

While the focus of this study of Catholic documents and teachings is language and moral argument, it would be misleading to think about these documents without reflecting on the powerful institution that stands behind them. Catholic sexual ethics integrate theological beliefs about God's created order with the belief that the Church has the authority to enforce order by commanding obedience from the laity. The created order reveals the moral norms that guide Catholic sexual activity and relationships. The individual knows her place in this order through her own reason, but Catholicism holds that she also needs the Church to clarify, interpret, and enforce this proper understanding. In these official documents, the Church gives orders/commands to the laity because it believes that those commands reflect the objective moral order and maintains it. Mark Jordan has said that in these Catholic documents, "The forces at work . . . are not only the forces of words." He claims that true change will not occur by amending documents, because "[c]hanging the language without reforming institutional arrangements would be useless, even if it were possible" (Jordan 2000, 4).

Regardless of whether one agrees with Jordan about the need for change in Catholic sexual ethics or about the most effective way to bring it about, his comments remind us of the connection between language and power. Rhetoric, he argues, distracts readers from content or argument because it moves readers to "opinion, passion, or action."[1] Rhetorical devices are dangerous because they resist analysis. Jordan proposes that to study them, one must "step aside from" the "glare" of this kind of speech and look instead "at it in rough reflection" (22). This requires an attitude of hostile suspicion toward these documents—he goes as far as characterizing them as "official hate speech." For Jordan, these documents cannot be trusted; one must put aside scholarly politeness and attack them with the attitude that they harbor something more sinister—"a particular structure of authority" (23).

Jordan's theologically motivated project is distinct from mine in this volume. I share his suspicion of rhetoric as well as his belief that all readers must view the words in Catholic documents in connection with the structures of authority that promulgate them. Nevertheless, I do not believe that the "attitude of hostile suspicion" he commends is necessary. My analysis requires a friendlier reading, mostly because I want to uncover the logic (or in some cases the lack of logic) in these documents. Thus, I have tried to adopt a unique posture toward them. To pick up on Jordan's language, I have exercised suspicion while maintaining scholarly politeness. I have given these documents the benefit of the doubt. This posture of polite suspicion is, I think, necessary when one reads religious documents from that odd place religious studies scholars try to carve out for ourselves. Catholic theology is distinct because the emphasis it places on human reason suggests that all reasonable people can read Catholic ethics and make sense of it. Indeed, most recent magisterial documents address all persons of goodwill precisely because of the belief that any human with the capacity for reason can penetrate these documents. The main reason I take these documents seriously is because I believe that they are not mere parochial documents. Indeed, recent developments have shown that what the Catholic Church teaches and does about sex has an impact on the wider public discourse about sex. Thus, all of us, citizens of the polis, must pay attention to these documents, even if the Church does not have such direct power over us. Nevertheless, even as I have read the documents politely, I have tried to take Jordan's concerns about the power of rhetoric seriously.

There is no doubt that structures of authority pervade the official Catholic teachings on marriage and reproduction. The primary goal of the teachings is to maintain order in its different dimensions. The order that is most at stake in these documents is the right relationship of male and female. Attitudes about gender are, in some sense, both the starting point and the endpoint of Catholic discourse about sex. In the view of the magisterium, God created the differentiation between male and female and the boundary that marks out this difference is not negotiable. Neither is the "natural" fact of the union between male and female—a union that is legitimate only when made sacred by the Church in marriage. Catholic marriage transforms sex into an activity of co-creation with God. Any sexual activity outside of this context is ruled out precisely because the Church views it as a turning away from God. By turning away, the individual also rejects the authority of the Church.

The Catholic documents' usage of gendered metaphors highlights the deep connection between institutional arrangements and language. I have tried to show that this practice cannot be ignored or simply written off as incidental to Catholic teaching. Indeed, these metaphors serve as clues that illuminate moral arguments on marriage and reproduction. By understanding the pervasiveness of gender as a socially constructed category that maintains order we can see the various relationships that Catholic sexual ethics emphasize more clearly: the relationship of self to God, the relationship of self to other, and the internal ordering of will to desire. A gendered analysis of these relations reveals that they all begin with the particular experience of each person as a gendered body. In Catholicism, gender complementarity is the way of describing the significance of that experience, and this metaphor of complementarity provides us with one way to explore the relationship of gender to sexuality or embodied states. The metaphorical use of the gendered female body to describe an entity such as the Church provides another interesting source that enables us to deepen our analysis of sexual ethics. These metaphors consistently depict the Church as fulfilling a role (wife, mother, virgin) defined by sexuality. How then does one reconcile this "sexing" of the Church with the rigid order imposed by its teaching on contraception and assisted reproduction? In other words, are the boundaries between male and female gender roles as impermeable as one might think at first blush? By thinking through these metaphors, we might begin to answer that question.

The fluidity of the boundaries between male and female gender roles has become an especially relevant issue of late. The two important issues in the contemporary public discussions of Catholicism and sex—same-sex marriage and sexual abuse of children by clerics—threaten the stability of these boundaries.[2] In this short conclusion, I hope to present some schematic reflections on how these issues relate to my larger project. In particular, I want to ask what, if anything, their prominence in public discourse at the beginning of the twenty-first century tells us about Catholic sexual ethics and gender attitudes.

The issue of same-sex marriage has moved to the forefront of both secular and religious discussion in the early twenty-first century. In early 2004, several legislative and judicial decisions in North America led to limited legal acceptance of same-sex unions and, in some cases, of same-sex marriage. The Catholic Church had addressed the broader issue of the morality of homosexuality in a series of documents in the 1980s and 1990s. These documents acknowledged the existence of a homosexual orientation but evaluated it as an objective disorder because of Catholicism's belief that it leads to acts that are by their very nature disordered (Grabowski 2003, 137). This disorder in the homosexual does not mean that the individual has less dignity or is somehow blameworthy for the orientation. The important point, however, is that a man or woman with a homosexual orientation cannot engage in any sexual activity with a person of the same sex. On this line of thinking, sexual continence is the only available option for a gay man or lesbian woman.

The salient distinction between a person's sexual orientation and the specific acts he or she engages in is a key element of the Church's condemnation of discrimination against homosexuals. John Grabowski argues that the "disorder" of homosexuality is not unique. He writes, "Indeed, as fallen, all men and women have inclinations that are disordered. What is morally relevant is whether a person acts on such disordered inclinations" (137). In the Catholic view, the chaste homosexual accepts and struggles with the burden of his or her fallenness, but other Catholics cannot use the fact of that fallenness as a reason to treat him or her unjustly.

The question of justice seems to be at the root of the debate about same-sex marriage. The issue is often framed as one of extending heterosexual rights to homosexuals. In the summer of 2003, the Vatican issued a document responding to this matter. *Considerations Regarding Proposals to Give Legal Recognition to Unions Between Homosexual Persons* describes itself as a reiteration of Catholic teachings on this issue and a presentation of "arguments drawn from reason" that will be useful to bishops as they address this question (Congregation for the Doctrine of Faith 2003, par. 1). The document strongly opposes homosexual unions of any type, and rejects the possibility that gay persons have a right to adopt children. The authors go as far as to say that "[a]llowing children to be adopted by persons living in such unions would actually mean doing violence to these children in the sense that their condition of dependency would be used to place them in an environment that is not conducive to their full human development" (par. 7). The use of natural law language is striking in this document, mainly because it is not accompanied by natural law arguments. The authors view the "natural moral law" as promulgating the self-evident premises that God established marriage and that the complementarity of the sexes is one of its central components. "No ideology can erase from the human spirit the certainty that marriage exists solely between a man and a woman" (par. 2). The document states this proclamation without offering an argument in its support.

The document begins with a statement about the nature, properties, and purpose of marriage; it only exists between man and woman and in cooperation with God leads to "the procreation and upbringing of new lives" (par. 2). According to the document, this is "evident to right reason," acknowledged "by all major cultures of the world," and "established by the Creator" (par. 2). Furthermore, scripture confirms this truth, mainly in the book of Genesis. This belief about marriage, combined with the belief that "homosexual acts go against the natural moral law," leads the Congregation for the Doctrine of Faith to conclude that "there are absolutely no grounds for considering homosexual unions to be in any way similar or even remotely analogous to God's plan for marriage and family" (par. 4).

The possibility of legally sanctioned same-sex marriage poses a serious threat to Catholic sexual ethics for obvious reasons—mainly because it violates the sacramental significance of marriage. This significance, as I have shown, is based on the belief that there is a strong distinction between male and female gender roles and the belief that each person needs another person of the opposite sex to achieve completion. Same-sex relations are in their very nature incomplete, and thus disordered, according to this view.

While the Church has responded quite directly to the issue of same-sex marriage, it has not yet developed into a crisis unique to the Church. Indeed, the Church's position does not appear to be unusual or marginal in the context of the debate in American culture at the moment. The prominence of the issue is the result of occurrences outside the Church. The clerical sexual-abuse scandal, by contrast, has led to a crisis in the Church brought about by the behavior of its own priests and bishops. The sexual abuse of children by priests is not a new phenomenon. What has changed in recent years is the willingness of victims to come forward with their stories and the revelation that these clerical abuses were not isolated incidents. Indeed, it has become quite clear that there has been a long-standing pattern of sexual misconduct by priests, especially toward children. Even more alarming to many is the pattern of denial and cover-up by the Church. Although there were isolated reports of clerical sexual misbehavior in the latter half of the twentieth century, the torrent of accusations and revelations in 2000–2003 were the most damning. A detailed investigation by the *Boston Globe* revealed the extent of this abuse. In the first three months of 2002, 190 investigative articles appeared in the *Globe,* and thousands more appeared in media outlets around the world (France 2004, 373).

The crisis that ensued is still being sorted out; however, certain preliminary observations are pertinent. American Catholics have responded to this crisis in a variety of ways, and the fact of this variety is interesting. Some (more-liberal Catholics) have seen this as an opportunity to question the structure of church authority and to revive what they see as the lost spirit of Vatican II with its emphasis on collegiality and openness. An example of this impulse has been the tremendous popularity of the group Voice of the Faithful, which organized in 2002 to address the Church's cover-up and mismanagement of the crisis, primarily in the Boston area. Others (more-conservative Catholics) have used this as an opportunity to blame society's lax sexual morality for the crisis. For example, in John Paul II's comments to the American Cardinals in Rome on April 23, 2002, he said, "The abuse of the young is a grave symptom of a crisis affecting not only the Church but society as a whole. It is a deep-seated crisis of sexual morality, even of human relationships, and its prime victims are the family and the young" (420). Thus, for some Catholics this issue revealed a deeper problem within the Church; for others it was the world outside that was to blame.

Same-sex marriage and clerical sexual abuse involve actions that the Church views as incidents of disorder because they violate God's created natural order and display disobedience to church authority. Catholic documents frequently describe homosexuality as disordered. The prospect of legitimate same-sex unions poses a serious challenge to the Catholic theology of marriage. The coherence of that theology depends on a certain view of order and on the cooperation of civil authorities in maintaining that order. The order of creation is, as we have noted, a reasonable (i.e., based on reason) one, even to non-Catholics. It is precisely for that reason that the Church cares so much about the state's response to same-sex unions.

The sexual-abuse scandals involve disorder at different levels—as disordered sexuality, as disobedience to the vow of celibacy, and as disorder in church governance. It is interesting that much of the Church's response to this scandal suggests that these clerical misdeeds are most notably instances of disobedience. This makes sense when one notices that the term used to describe the priesthood is often described as "the sacrament of the holy orders." Priests are ordained to the holy orders by vowing to be obedient. The Catechism asks the direct question "why is this sacrament called 'orders'?" Its response is to trace the word "order" to Roman antiquity where it referred to an "established civil body, especially a governing body" (United States Catholic Conference 1994, 1537). Ordination, then, is the act of integrating a person into the body—the order. Order is the body, and the body is the community—more specifically, it is the governing body. The consecrated individual takes a vow to enter a body and denies his or her own body to exemplify the ultimate order—the holy order. Priests who break the vow of celibacy and, more seriously, priests who harm children do violence to the body of the Church. Their action is not merely disobedient to authority but also willfully violent toward it. What is particularly troubling, however, is the way that the Church (understood here as the governing bishops) knew of this disobedience and violence and did nothing to stop it.

The obedience of the priest to his "holy order" is ultimately obedience to God. From the perspective of Catholicism, the type of order most relevant to sexual morality is the proper attitude of the Christian to God. Being in right relation to God means that God's grace will assist the individual in controlling passions. Pope Pius XI emphasizes this point in *Casti Connubii*:

For it is a sacred ordinance that whoever shall have first subjected himself to God will, by the aid of divine grace, be glad to subject his own passions and concupiscence; while he who is a rebel against God will, to his sorrow, experience within himself the violent rebellion of his worst passions. (Pius XI 1930, 50–51)

Thus, in a theological sense, these priests have rebelled against God, and through that rebellion they have brought about the most profound disorder. While I think it is dangerous to equate the "disorder" of homosexuality with the "disorder" of sexual abuse, it appears that the Catholic logic of order leads precisely to that conclusion.

These issues are relevant to our reflections on gender, the other organizing focus of this volume. In fact, the orders I have explored in this book all ultimately rest on the order of gender. Attitudes about gender support the authority of the Church and the authority of its moral teachings. Feminine descriptions of the Church have helped us understand Catholic attitudes about gender and sex. I think that the prevalence of the two issues of same-sex marriage and clerical sexual abuse can do similar work. Clerical sexual abuse has been identified largely with male sexuality and male identity. The issue of same-sex marriages affects both men and women, so in some sense it appears to transcend gender. The Church, of course, would not view it as a transcendence of gender but rather as a willful rejection of the order maintained by gender roles. To accept homosexuality as morally licit and to legitimize same-sex unions would undermine the order of complementarity because it would acknowledge that other ordered sexual relationships are possible. The clerical sexual abuse scandal, by contrast, defies the logic of order altogether. Preying on young children and using them as sexual objects is outside the order of meaningful human relationships.

Catholic attitudes about same-sex marriages and priestly sexual abuse point to the convergence of two Catholic impulses—the ordered nature of God's creation and the importance of obedience to church hierarchy. Catholic teaching prescribes sexual abstinence for all homosexuals. By distinguishing between a homosexual identity and a homosexual act, the Church has effectively imposed chastity on those who desire someone of the same sex. By disciplining these desires, the Church believes that it maintains the natural orders of procreative sex and gender complementarity. Yet instead of relying exclusively on the language of order and creation, the magisterium turns to a very different mode of moral discourse in its 2003 document on same-sex unions, emphasizing the consequences of these unions on societal structures.

The persistent practices of privileging celibacy and calling the Church female have taken a toll on the Catholic priesthood. Although I am not qualified to comment on the causes of priestly sexual abuse—a topic that is much debated—it seems plausible to suggest that celibacy and gendered metaphors might contribute to priestly formation and perhaps even behavior. The sex-abuse scandals, which include both the acts perpetuated by priests and the apparent cover-ups by the hierarchy, have shaken the Catholic order in a variety of ways. One can use the language of sin or the language of crime to describe the offending priests' actions—either way, their actions disrupt the order. One can only imagine that from the perspective of their victims, young boys and girls who placed their trust in that order, the rupture was irreparable. One male victim interviewed by David France describes the effect of the abuse he suffered as teaching him "that the church was not the literal 'Bride of Christ' he had been taught, but a temporal network of buildings, good values, and well-meaning men who so badly wanted him to believe this mystical heaven-on-earth thing that they compounded one horrendous decision with another to keep him from glimpsing the first little flaw. The flaw of hubris" (France 2004, 436). This victim's belief that the Church was female (bride) in relation to the male Christ was shattered when a male priest who represented the Church violated him sexually. The complex layers of belief about gender and sex evident in this one statement speak for themselves.

These two pressing matters—the Church's response to gay persons who want to sacralize their commitment to one another and its response to sexual misconduct among those who have vowed to be celibate—are matters that will occupy Catholic theologians for a long time. I simply note that the prominence of these issues in public discourse about Catholicism and sex provides evidence that sexual doctrines and attitudes about gender are intimately connected to church authority in a way that ensures the Church's power both to interpret and enforce order in the lives of all Catholics.

I. Order and Sexual Ethics

1. Kathleen Sands argues that the contemporary phenomenon where "sex and reproduction are taken as the central concerns of religion" is the result of the economic and social power of the religious right (Sands 2000, 5). In other words, religious conservatives have succeeded in making "family values" synonymous with religious values. Sands argues that the danger of this view is that when family becomes the locus of religion, issues of social justice and politics are ignored. Thus, religious views about justice and the economy are rendered irrelevant, whereas religious teachings about the family (sexuality and reproduction) are seen as uncontroversial.

2. I am aware of the long history of the use of order in theological ethics, especially in the context of the distinction between created order and redemptive order. While that traditional usage of the concept bears some resemblance to mine, I am not interested in exploring the way that distinction works in Catholicism. Clearly, similar pairs such as nature/grace and law/gospel are also important to theological ethics.

3. See Augustine, *City of God,* book 13, chapter 13.

4. See Gudorf 1988 for a more detailed treatment of this shift.

5. The equality espoused in contemporary Catholicism is connected to the created order but not necessarily to the redemptive order as evidenced in the Church's continued support of a male-only priesthood. Rosemary Radford Ruether has referred to this as "a contradiction between anthropology and Christology"—a trend that she notes exists in contemporary official Catholic documents (Ruether 1991, 98).

NOTES

6. He is rephrasing Augustine's own definition of order in *The City of God.* There Augustine writes that "order is the distribution which allots things equal and unequal, each to its own place" (bk. 19, ch. 13).

7. Curran attributes the term "sacramentality" to Richard P. McBrien and "analogical imagination" to David Tracy (Curran 1999).

8. The terms "sex," "gender," and "sexuality" are all controversial. Many have noted that the approach, which I embrace here, of associating gender with cultural construction and sex with physical structure simply reinforces a dangerous dichotomy. In his book *The Ethics of Sex,* Mark Jordan adopts the practice of using the terms interchangeably and uses the term "sex" "vaguely and inclusively" to include sexuality and gender. He thinks, for example, that the terms sex and gender are "ambiguously physical and cultural, determined

and determinable" (Jordan 2002, 14). I discuss the debates about terminology at greater length later in this chapter.

9. Excellent studies include Rosemary Radford Ruether's *Sexism and God Talk,* and Elizabeth Schüssler Fiorenza's *In Memory of Her.*

10. While this claim is difficult to verify, there is much in Catholic culture that romanticizes maternity and even expressly suggests that women are only truly fulfilled through motherhood.

11. See Ryan 2001 for more on the difficulties faced by Catholic couples, especially chapter 6, "Faith and Infertility."

12. Jordan claims that "one of the things that distinguishes Christian sexual ethics is the way it mobilizes power around sex" (Jordan 2002, 19).

13. Judith Plaskow, commenting about Judaism, writes, "Wherever we look in Jewish sources, it is clear that the regulation of women's sexuality is absolutely fundamental to women's oppression" (Plaskow 2000, 24).

14. Susan Ross's work in several articles, as well as in her book, has influenced much of my thinking on these issues. See Ross 1991, 1992, and 1998.

2. THEOLOGY AND MARRIAGE

1. For more-sustained historical accounts see Mackin 1982.

2. "It is reasonably accurate to see the beginning of the modern era of Catholic teaching on marriage the sacrament in Pope Leo XIII's encyclical letter, *Arcanum divinae sapientiae,* of February 10, 1880," writes Mackin in his thorough treatment of this issue (Mackin 1989, 516).

3. Noonan participated in meetings of the Papal Birth Control Commission convened in the mid-1960s to advise the Vatican on contraception. In 1965, he lectured to the commission on the history of the Church's view on contraception and concluded that "church teaching on this question had gradually changed, impelled by varying conditions of the times, and always with a view toward preserving basic respect for human life" (Kaiser 1985, 82). Also, it is important to note that John Henry Cardinal Newman's *An Essay on the Development of Christian Doctrine* influenced Noonan's view about the development of doctrine. In 1993, Noonan published an article that explicitly adapts Newman's approach to change. Newman had explained "the apparent variation and growth of doctrine" in Christianity as a necessary part of any "philosophy or polity which takes possession of the intellect and heart, and has had any wide or extended dominion" (Newman 1989, 29). This necessity emerges from the human need to absorb and comprehend ideas slowly. According to Newman, all the wonderful truth of Christianity "could not be comprehended all at once by the recipients"; they "required only the longer time and deeper thought for their full elucidation" (301). This explanation does not map perfectly onto Noonan's depiction of more-abrupt change in moral doctrine. Noonan does, however, embrace one reference in Newman's essay to change as emerging from a conflict of ideas against the background

of an objective principle. For Noonan, "that principle of change is the person of Christ" (Noonan 1993, 677).

4. Ross acknowledges that she is drawing on Richard McBrien's analysis of sacraments.

5. The language of essential properties is replaced by the language of purposes, meanings, and ends in later magisterial writings. However, in one passage, Leo XIII asks to what purpose marriage tends (he also refers to the fruits of marriage, as opposed to its essential attributes or properties). He responds that it is intended for the propagation of the human race and for making the lives of married persons more virtuous and happier (mutual assistance to relieve necessities, constant and faithful love, the community of all possessions). The stress of this document, however, is on the attributes or properties of marriage, not its purposes or goals. The practical topic it addresses is divorce rather than procreation. In *Rerum Novarum*, Leo's most well-known encyclical, he emphasizes the primacy of procreation: "No human law can abolish the natural and primitive right of marriage, or in any way limit the chief and principal purpose of marriage, ordained by God's authority from the beginning. 'Increase and multiply' " (O'Brien and Shannon 1992, 18).

6. John 2:1–11.

7. The interesting upshot of this view is that even non-Christians who are married violate the primeval law if they break the bond. In *Casti* we read, "Therefore, although the sacramental element may be absent from a marriage as is the case among unbelievers, still in such a marriage, inasmuch as it is a true marriage there must remain and indeed there does remain the perpetual bond which by divine right is so bound up with matrimony from its first institution that it is not subject to any civil power" (Pius XI 1930, 18).

8. In addition to the more-official exhortations and magisterial documents, John Paul II has reflected on marriage and sexuality in a series of other writings and speeches. His 1960 work *Love and Responsibility* is a detailed study of human sexuality based on his years of pastoral experience: "It is not an exposition of doctrine. It is, rather, the result above all of an incessant confrontation of doctrine with life" (Wojtyla 1960, 15). After becoming pope in 1979, John Paul II expanded his views in a series of audiences on this issue. These have been collected in a volume entitled *The Theology of the Body: Human Love in the Divine Plan* (John Paul II 1997).

9. "Therefore a man leaves his father and his mother and cleaves to his wife, and they become one flesh" (Genesis 2:24). "Be subject to one another out of reverence for Christ. Wives, be subject to your husbands, as to the Lord. For the husband is the head of the wife as Christ is the head of the Church, his body, and is himself its savior" (Ephesians 5:21–23).

10. In the Congregation for the Doctrine of Faith's *Declaration on Sexual Ethics,* we read, "[T]he moral order of sexuality involves such high values of human life that every direct violation of this order is objectively serious" (Congregation for the Doctrine of Faith 1975, X).

11. Rogers argues against this particular reading of the tradition on several grounds. First, he claims that procreation as a good "belongs to the species" rather than to "the couple as such" (Rogers 1999, 205). This claim supports the view that not every human being must accomplish reproduction. Since Rogers's purpose is to provide a Christian justification for same-sex marriage, the allowance and positive valuation of celibacy points to the fact that procreation cannot be the primary good for every human being. Hence, "the human does not *need* procreation to fulfill the image of God any more than God *needs* creation to be the Trinity" (205). For Rogers, God's creative acts are less a necessity than they are "acts of self-determining love." In other words, choosing to love another in the covenant of marriage is a better analogy of "God's self-determining love in creation" than is procreation (207).

12. Pius XI makes explicit reference to St. Augustine's threefold formula and also quotes him extensively to show how these blessings of marriage contain "a splendid summary of the whole doctrine of Christian marriage" (Pius XI 1930, 8).

13. Noonan notes that the Anglican decision was just the first in a remarkable shift most Protestant denominations made on this issue; see Noonan 1965, 490.

14. The concept of a lay apostolate has existed in Catholicism for much of its history. In 1965, the Second Vatican Council issued *Apostolicam Actuositatem* (*Decree on the Apostolate of the Laity*). "Apostolate" is defined as a sharing in the priestly, prophetic, and royal office of Christ. *Apostolicam* uses the imagery of the relationship of parts to whole to emphasize this important role for the laity: "Indeed so intimately are the parts linked and interrelated in this body (cf. Eph. 4:16) that the member who fails to make his [*sic*] proper contribution to the development of the Church must be said to be useful neither to the Church nor to himself [*sic*]" (Abbott 1966, 491).

15. Ford and Kelly were significant players in the interpretation of Catholic moral theology in the United States in the 1950s and 1960s. As editors of the journal *Theological Studies,* they commented regularly on contemporary moral problems. By some accounts, John Ford was instrumental in composing *Humanae Vitae*. See Kaiser 1985 for more detail on Ford's role in the issuance of the encyclical.

Ford also published a landmark article in 1942, "Marriage: Its Meaning and Purposes." In the article, he takes on Herbert Doms's theory that "marriage has a meaning, or inherent value, which is present independently of the purposes to which marriage is naturally orientated" (Ford 1942, 335). Ford rejects Doms's insistence on the distinction between meanings and ends of marriage. He writes, "[T]he ends of marriage are its meanings" (366). Ford also mounts a defense of the "language of primary and secondary ends" both because it is the official language of the Church and because it is justified (368).

16. Several terms are used, often synonymously, to describe the appropriate ordering of sexual desires. In addition to chastity, we note continence, celibacy,

and virginity. Clearly these terms refer to different statuses or practices. Nevertheless, they all concern the control and regulation of sexuality.

17. "Marriage and virginity or celibacy are two ways of expressing and living the one mystery of the covenant of God with his people" (John Paul II 1981, 16).

18. Christine Gudorf argues that the Augustinian view that sexual pleasure is dangerous "because it is virtually irresistible" is misguided and is the root of Christianity's nervousness about sexual pleasure. She explores the argument about the irresistibility of sexual pleasure, describing it as a loss of control that "lures us into a focus on our individual satisfaction, and therefore tempts us to be selfish, to ignore or abuse others" (Gudorf 1994, 83). She concludes that the irresistibility argument is based on an inaccuracy; that in reality, resisting and postponing sexual pleasure is a frequent practice. Furthermore, she claims that this argument is dangerous when used to justify sexual aggression such as rape and harassment, especially since the argument is applied to men and women differently.

19. For an interesting discussion of sex within marriage in the history of Christian ethics, see Jordan 2002, 107–130.

20. The tradition of Catholic social teaching has stressed the living wage and its importance in maintaining family stability. In O'Brien and Shannon, see *Rerum Novarum,* par. 35; *Quadragesimo Anno,* par. 70; *Mater et Magistra,* par. 71; and *Laborem Excerens,* par. 19. Another influential source in this discussion of families and living wages is the work of John A. Ryan (1920).

21. In the encyclical letter *Sacra Virginitas* [*On Holy Virginity*], Pius XII describes the advantages of consecrated celibacy and notes its ambiguous relationship to sexual pleasure. He acknowledges that "the renouncement of all sexual pleasure" leads to spiritual advances. However, "It is not to be thought that such pleasure, when it arises from lawful marriage, is reprehensible in itself; on the contrary, the chaste use of marriage is ennobled and sanctified. . . . Nevertheless, it must be equally admitted that as a consequence of the fall of Adam the lower faculties of human nature are no longer obedient to right reason, and may involve man in dishonorable actions" (Liebard 1978, 140).

22. See Curran 1992, 25, for a discussion of physicalism.

3. Reproduction

1. The official press release of the National Catholic Welfare Conference on that day describes the scene as follows: "Coffee bars were virtually deserted and council Fathers listened in silence as debate began on marriage and the family" (Anderson 1965–1966, 206).

2. McClory's account of the commission presents Cardinal Leo Joseph Suenens as "the person most responsible for the creation of the Birth Control Commission" (McClory 1995, 38). Suenens, the archbishop of Malines-Brussels, Belgium, convened a series of informal conferences at the University

of Louvain in the late 1950s to explore the issue further. These conferences, attended by participants from various walks of life, became a model for the Papal Birth Control Commission. According to McClory, Suenens (who by the early 1960s had been elevated to cardinal) suggested the commission to Pope John XXIII mainly because of fears that the Vatican Council would simply reaffirm the traditional teaching and that such a reaffirmation might "attain a kind of immortality" as conciliar doctrine. McClory does admit that an even more persuasive factor for John XXIII to convene the commission was the UN and WHO conference on world population slated for mid-1964. In McClory's words, "The Vatican feared the sort of sweeping recommendations for population control that might come from such an event" (1995, 41).

3. Saigh's impatient and angry speech displayed an urgency that led him to utter one of the most well-known lines to come from these debates: "[D]o we not have the right to ask ourselves whether certain official positions are not subordinated to obsolete conceptions and possibly even to the psychosis of bachelors who are strangers to this sector of life?" (Anderson 1965–1966, 209).

4. To the question of whether the use of the birth control pill was licit, Pius XII stated in 1958 in an address to the Seventh International Hematological Congress in Rome, "The answer depends on the intention of the person. If a woman takes such medicine, not to prevent conception, but only on the advice of a doctor as a necessary remedy because of the condition of the uterus or the organism, she produces *indirect* sterilization, which is permitted according to general principles governing acts with a double effect. But a *direct* and, therefore, illicit sterilization results when ovulation is stopped to protect the uterus and the organisms from the consequences of a pregnancy which it is not able to sustain. Some moralists contend that it is permissible to take medicines with this later intention, but they are in error" (Liebard 1978, 237).

5. A footnote in *Gaudium et Spes* describes Pope John XXIII's move: "Certain questions which need further and more careful investigation have been handed over, at the command of the Supreme Pontiff, to a commission for the study of population, family and births, in order that, after it fulfills its function, the Supreme Pontiff may pass judgment" (Abbott 1966, 256). This appeared to leave open the possibility that the pope was considering changing the teaching. In this same footnote, however, the council authors cited Pius XI's encyclical and Pius XII's address to the midwives as a way to emphasize the force and consistency of tradition.

6. Bernard Häring's commentary on *Gaudium et Spes*'s treatment of marriage and family describes the shift as a solid rejection of "the older teaching about the 'ends of marriage.' " He writes, "[T]he Council decided after long discussion to describe first the fundamental nature of marriage as a covenant of love, thus making it clear that love is not merely subjective supplement to the objective, divinely established 'ends' but is, as it were, the root or stem

from which truly human, generous fecundity is to be expected" (Häring 1967, 237).

7. The report issued by the Papal Birth Control Commission several years later relies on this language of "objective standards." See McClory 1995, 171–187.

8. The six-member papal commission that Pope John XXIII convened in 1963 consisted of a blend of clergy and lay members. By the fourth meeting in 1965, the commission had grown to include thirty-four laypersons, including five women. In fact, the laypersons outnumbered the clergy. But, in what McClory describes as an "unexplained procedural shift," the Vatican changed the status of the lay members for the last session in 1966. They were essentially demoted from members to "experts," which meant that they could not vote on the final draft. The only voting members were sixteen cardinals and bishops appointed by the pope. McClory suspects that this happened because some of the clergy on the commission sensed that the tide was turning toward acceptance of contraception and thought they could avert change by limiting the voting membership. Whatever the true reasons for the change in membership, when the sixteen-member commission of bishops and cardinals voted, their responses were in favor of accepting contraception as licit.

9. Chapter 3 of *Lumen Gentium* (Abbott 1966, 37–56) reveals the ambiguous characterization of collegiality. While individual bishops have a great deal of power, *Lumen Gentium* claims that "the college or body of bishops has no authority unless it is simultaneously conceived of in terms of its head, the Roman Pontiff, Peter's successor, and without lessening of his power of primacy over all, pastors as well as the general faithful" (Abbott 1966, 43).

10. The final report is often referred to as the majority report and is contrasted with the so-called minority report. McClory describes the minority report as "an unauthorized, alternative report." According to his account, the commission had only agreed to present their final report to the pope, but Cardinal Ottaviani, John Ford, and the other theologians (Visser, Zalba, and Lestapis) who had opposed the commission's report wanted their viewpoint represented; see McClory 1995, 110–111, 129–130.

11. The language of physical evil and good (and the associated terms "ontic," "premoral evil," and "good") is a central element of the proportionalist approach to moral norms. Proportionalists rely on this distinction to make the claim that conflicts between various goods are not all the same. They argue that often the values in conflict are of a premoral sort and thus can be overridden for the sake of another value. The resulting evil is then characterized as a physical or premoral evil. For an in-depth discussion, see Jannsens 1979 and Hoose 1987.

12. One of the central issues in the Catholic debate about proportionalist method in moral reasoning has been the use of a utilitarian-like reasoning. For an excellent treatment of this question, see Cahill 1981.

13. All this is taken from Robert McClory's account. McClory is quoting from the National Catholic News Service, August 8, 1968.

14. The primary defenders of the view that *Humanae Vitae* was an infallible document are John Ford, S.J., and Germain Grisez. Their claim rests on the point that Vatican II "reaffirmed the possibility of infallibility in the exercise of the ordinary magisterium [the bishops]" (Ford and Grisez 1988, 125).

15. See Horgan 1972.

16. In an interesting article, Paul Lauritzen draws attention to the contrast between Catholic responses to reproductive technology and Catholic responses to abortion, cloning, and stem-cell research. According to Catholic teaching, all three practices are morally prohibited, but as Lauritzen notes, the rhetoric surrounding Catholic opposition to reproductive technologies is muted when compared to other issues that involve potential harm to the embryo. See Lauritzen 2003.

17. One interesting footnote to this history occurred in the short papacy of John Paul I. Apparently, he sent his congratulations to the couple that gave birth to the first test-tube baby in 1979 (Wills 2000, 97).

18. The rise in political importance of abortion has led to an increased focus on the embryo. In the early twenty-first century, the rhetoric surrounding protection of the embryo has become even stronger. See Lauritzen 2003.

19. Catholic doctrines consider prenatal diagnosis morally licit if it "respects the life and integrity of the embryo and the human fetus and is directed toward its safeguarding or healing as an individual." Similarly, therapeutic genetic intervention must meet the criteria of respecting the life and integrity of the embryo by not exposing it to disproportionate risks if it is to be considered licit. In both cases, the telos must be healing, improved health, or survival. See Congregation for the Doctrine of Faith 1987, I.2 and 3.

20. See, for example, John Paul II's address on November 10, 2003, to the Pontifical Academy of Sciences.

21. On the basis of these anthropological and normative claims, *Donum Vitae* makes a practical claim that the effect of any intervention on the human body involves the entire person on different levels. Thus, all physical/medical interventions have a moral dimension; they all entail a potential assault on the dignity of the person or, in the case of therapeutic interventions, a benefit. Hence, as creatures of God, persons are due respect in both their bodily and spiritual dimensions. This "somatic-spiritual unity" was emphasized in a 1985 apostolic letter, *Dolentium Hominum*. There, John Paul II affirms that health affects more than the person's physical body. He notes that medicine cannot fully capture the questions raised by the experience of illness and suffering. These are phenomena that "touch the essence of the human condition in this world" (John Paul II 1985, 2).

22. See McCormick 1990 and Coughlan 1990. Both fault the instruction for conflating "genetic identity" with "personal identity" in its discussion of the moral status of the embryo.

23. The magisterium also uses this argument to claim that homosexual couples cannot adopt children. The Congregation for the Doctrine of Faith writes, "As experience has shown, the absence of sexual complementarity in these

unions creates obstacles in the normal development of children who would be placed in the care of such [homosexual] persons" (Congregation for the Doctrine of Faith 2003, par. 7).

24. See Cahill and Shannon 1968, 118–132 for a helpful discussion of American responses to the Vatican's instruction.

25. The authority of the two documents is different. *Humanae Vitae* is a papal encyclical, while *Donum Vitae* is an instruction issued by the Congregation for the Doctrine of Faith, a part of the Roman Curia.

26. The matter of terminology is very tricky in this area. I rely on "artificial contraception" and "assisted reproduction" because I believe they most adequately reflect the activities they represent.

27. This terminology is significant, since Catholic defenders of the Church's teaching on contraception reject the former and embrace the latter. Referring to this method as "natural" certainly adds to the perception that Catholicism rejects the nonnatural—a perception that is not accurate.

28. Canon Law Society of America, Canon 1084.

29. See Kalbian 2002.

30. See Joseph Selling's excellent article on the historical development of this concept. He argues that Paul VI's claim in the encyclical that church teaching on marriage has been "proposed with constant firmness" is inaccurate. He illustrates how the history of church teaching on conjugal morality (especially in the twentieth century) has been one of innovation, especially in the area of the ends of marriage. Selling concludes that until *Humanae Vitae,* the tradition displayed "an ever expanding understanding of the meanings or purposes of sexual relations within marriage." *Humanae Vitae* signals a contraction on this issue and, in Selling's view, an innovation (Selling 1998, 29–31).

31. Cristina Traina offers a helpful description of personalism in her book *Feminist Ethics and Natural Law.* See Traina 1999, 106–113.

32. Leonhard Weber remarks that "[I]t is not said why this connection is inseparable and why man must not intervene and control precisely in this matter" (Weber 1967, 398).

33. A fascinating resource in this regard is the volume *The Experience of Marriage: The Testimony of Catholic Laymen,* ed. Michael Novak, a compilation of first-person testimonies from married Catholic men and women about their experiences in marriage especially as they relate to birth control and procreation. While the book must be read in the context of the Vatican II–era discussions about contraception, it offers a perspective on the powerful role of experience in moral reasoning.

34. See Secker 1993.

35. We can also chart the development of the principle of totality by exploring Pius XII's use of it in moral judgments about impotence and in vitro fertilization. In the 1940s and 1950s, it was a central principle in debates about the moral justification of organ donation.

4. GENDER

1. The work of Susan Ross is noteworthy on this topic, especially on the nuptial metaphor. See Ross 1991 and 1998.

2. The most prominent biblical example is Ephesians 5:25.

3. Häring writes, "The encyclical *Humanae Vitae* reaffirms the positive value of the marital act as expressive of conjugal love; such valuation was not at all common before St. Alphonsus of Liguori, or even before Pius XII and Vatican II" (Häring 1993, 154).

4. "Man and woman are called from the beginning not only to exist 'side by side' or 'together,' but they are also called *to exist mutually 'one for the other'* " (John Paul II 1988, par. 7).

5. Ross uses the language of completion to describe the relationship of genders in the gender-complementarity model; see Ross 2001, 40.

6. Ross notes that the twentieth-century move to personalist language and criteria in the theology of marriage poses a challenge to "the hierarchical structure of marriage and, by analogy . . . the hierarchical structure of the Church" (Ross 1991, 347). The ultimate acceptance of this less-hierarchical model of marriage could only occur when a theory of complementarity between the sexes was established. In other words, the move to inseparability of ends was dependent on the more egalitarian view of gender relations offered by the complementarity model.

7. Ross bases this characterization on John Paul II's interpretation of gender complementarity, particularly as expressed in his 1988 apostolic letter *Mulieres Dignitatem*. See Ross 2001, 40.

8. There appear to be weaker and stronger versions of gender complementarity. The common thread in all versions is the belief that male and female are of equal value in the eyes of God and that their human dignity ought to be protected equally. The stronger versions refer to how much emphasis is placed on the difference between male and female roles and on the rigidity of the assigned gender roles. In its strongest version, gender complementarity is the claim that men and women have essential, unchangeable roles and that any transgressions of those roles violate a deep and eternal order. The weaker version stresses equality and interdependence and downplays gender-role stereotyping. There is evidence that both versions have informed recent Catholic theology of family, marriage, and sexuality.

9. Gudorf identifies what she calls a "schizophrenic quality" in Pope John Paul II's teaching on women. According to Gudorf, his social teachings on the role of women in the private realm display a greater emphasis on justice and equality than do his teachings on women's role in the family and marriage; see Gudorf 1988, 66. She also notes that the less-positive treatment of women is found in his "less well-known sermons and addresses, especially in more devotional speeches on Mary and the saints, and in addresses to local groups" (67–68). Gudorf suggests that while John Paul II supports the equality of the sexes on an intellectual level, his personal spirituality, especially in the form

of devotion to Mary, leads him to press for a more traditional femininity. Often the seemingly positive emphasis on women's "special" gifts obscures that traditional view. Women are held up to a morally superior status, one that is linked to an inherent quality. In this construction, women who attempt to undermine the natural order are perceived as undermining themselves.

10. Ross suggests that John Paul II's reading of the creation narrative "elides the P (Priestly) and the J (Jahwist) stories" (Ross 2001, 44). I agree with Ross that he elides the two stories, especially in the sense that he never resolves some of the apparent tensions between the two. It is clear, however, that he focuses mostly on the J stories because of what he sees as a mythological richness that reveals layers of deeper meaning. As Ross and others have noted, John Paul II's mode of exegesis is heavily influenced by that of Hans Urs von Balthasar.

11. In *Mulieres Dignitatem,* he is even more explicit about his views of the two creation accounts. He states, "[W]e find no essential contradiction between the two texts. The text of Genesis 2:18–25 helps us to understand better what we find in the concise passage of Genesis 1:27–28" (John Paul II 1988, par. 6).

12. "So, God-Yahweh says: 'It is not good that the man should be alone; I will make him a helper fit for him' " (Genesis 2:18). Quoted in John Paul II 1997, 43.

13. See also Ross 2001, 41.

14. Ross notes further evidence of this dichotomy by comparing the way Catholic documents understand male and female sexual behavior before and after marriage. She notes a shift in the theological anthropology of male and female from the "courtship" (premarital) phase to the marriage phase. Many of the pre–Vatican II pastoral treatises on marriage and sexuality emphasize women's purity and spirituality in the courtship phase, whereas in marriage, physicality and materiality come to reside almost solely in the female. This is clearest in the belief that before marriage, the focus is on controlling male sexuality, which the documents perceive as more potent. After marriage, the focus shifts to women's role in reproduction. Ross writes, "[I]n courtship it is the woman's (spiritual) responsibility to lead the man away from his physical desires, but in marriage it is the man's (spiritual) responsibility to lead the woman away from her limited focus on the material world, especially babies and children" (Ross 1991, 350–351).

15. She contrasts this to the more positive view expressed by Jesus that "women will be saved and venerated . . . for their participation in the larger project of the Kingdom of God in Luke 11:27–28" (Gudorf 1988, 70).

16. Melady is influenced by the work of Roderick Hart, George Lakoff, and Mark Johnson on this issue.

17. There is a long history of aligning the Church with maternal and other feminine metaphors. See the works of Joseph C. Plumpe and Karl Delhaye for careful studies of the patristic era. Avery Dulles, S.J., offers an important look at the contemporary significance of models of the Church.

18. Dulles makes this point effectively in *Models of the Church*. He writes that biblical images of the Church "suggest attitudes and courses of action; they intensify confidence and devotion. To some extent they are self-fulfilling; they make the Church become what they suggest the Church is" (Dulles 1974, 18).

19. As I have noted, the maternal metaphor for the Church is one of the oldest. Plumpe dates the earliest preserved instance of this usage to 177 c.e. from the *Epistola Ecclesiarum Viennensis et Lugdunensis*. The letters recount the martyrdom of the Christians of Lyons; see Plumpe, 36–37. *Lumen Gentium* attributes the use of these maternal metaphors to St. Ambrose of Milan. See Abbott 1966, 92.

20. The notion of a democratic Catholic Church is championed by many theologians in the volume *A Democratic Catholic Church,* edited by Bianchi and Ruether.

21. "Wives, be subject to your husbands, as to the Lord. For the husband is the head of the wife" (Ephesians 5:22–23).

22. This quote also appears in *Lumen Gentium,* paragraph 56. See Abbott 1966, 88.

23. Maurice Hammington suggests that in the Jewish tradition, as described in the Hebrew Scriptures, virginity was an economic consideration. Since women were viewed as property belonging either to their fathers or to their husbands, evidence of virginity before marriage was crucial to preserving the purity of family lineage. Hammington also suggests that the Catholic doctrine of Mary's virginity transforms the concept "from an economic consideration to a sacred religious consideration" (Hammington 1995, 55).

24. *Mater et Magistra* is not an encyclical about sex and marriage. There is, however, a reference to birth control in the section "Population Increase and Economic Development." Here, John XXIII dismisses claims that there is a threat to society from a population increase: "God in his goodness and wisdom has, on the one hand, provided nature with almost inexhaustible productive capacity; and, on the other hand, has endowed man with such ingenuity that, by using suitable means, he can apply nature's resources to the need and requirements of existence" (O'Brien and Shannon 1992, 115). Thus, the emphasis ought to be in providing for more people rather than on finding ways to limit population growth. He expresses opposition to contraceptive practices by deeming them to be violations of the laws of nature and God's creative plan.

25. The contrast between a merciful, compassionate mother Church and a harsh and rigid magisterium is present in another form in the Catholic tradition. Elizabeth Johnson, C.S.J., notes certain medieval aberrations "which envisioned Mary as the zone of mercy over and against Christ or God the Father, angry and just judges needing to be placated" (Johnson 1992, 97). The patriarchal family is premised on the presence of these roles; the mother is needed to intercede on behalf of the children.

26. James F. Childress has commented on the various metaphors at work

in this encyclical. He focuses especially on the war metaphors. See Childress 1997, 28–32.

27. One frustration with the documents is that they never fully acknowledge direct guilt for what happened or what may have failed to happen. I argued in an earlier paper that the metaphors used in these documents obscure the issue of responsibility; see Kalbian 2001.

28. See Plumpe 1943 and Delhaye 1964.

29. He proposes instead the use of the metaphor "pilgrim people of God," which was the one favored by the authors of *Lumen Gentium* (Sullivan 2000, 17–22).

30. He does emphasize however that the "the Church's motherhood can never in fact be separated from her teaching mission" (John Paul II 1993, 117).

31. See the Congregation for the Doctrine of the Faith's *Letter to the Bishops of the Catholic Church on the Pastoral Care of Homosexual Persons* in Gramick and Furey 1988, 1–10.

5. CONCLUSION

1. He identifies several of the dangerous modes of official Catholic rhetoric on the morality of homosexuality: "numbing repetition that impoverishes language," "the invocation of absolute authorities," "the making of violent threats" (Jordan 2000, 22).

2. Instead of these two issues, I chose to focus my study on marriage and reproduction for two reasons. First, Catholic sexual ethics bases itself on the notions that marriage is the only legitimate locus of sexual activity and that reproduction (procreation) must always be intended (at least in some sense) as a possible outcome. Second, the metaphors I explored in chapter 4 mainly use feminine marital and reproductive images to describe the Church.

Abbott, Walter M., S.J., ed. 1966. *The Documents of Vatican II.* The America Press, Geoffrey Chapman.

Anderson, Floyd, ed. 1965–1966. *Council Daybook, Vatican II, Session 1-4.* Washington, D.C.: National Catholic Welfare Conference.

Augustine, St. 1998. *The City of God against the Pagans.* Edited and translated by R. W. Dyson. New York: Cambridge University Press.

Bianchi, Eugene C., and Rosemary Radford Ruether. 1992. *A Democratic Catholic Church: The Reconstruction of Roman Catholicism.* New York: Crossroad.

Butler, Judith. 1990. *Gender Trouble: Feminism and the Subversion of Identity.* New York: Routledge.

Bynum, Caroline Walker. 1982. *Jesus as Mother: Studies in the Spirituality of the High Middle Ages.* Berkeley: University of California Press.

Bynum, Caroline Walker, Stevan Harrell, and Paula Richman, eds. 1986. *Gender and Religion: On the Complexity of Symbols.* Boston: Beacon Press.

Cahill, Lisa Sowle. 1981. "Teleology, Utilitarianism, and Christian Ethics." *Theological Studies* 42: 601–629.

———. 1985. *Between the Sexes: Foundations for a Christian Ethics of Sexuality.* Philadelphia: Fortress Press.

———. 1992. *Women and Sexuality.* New York: Paulist Press.

———. 1996. *Sex, Gender, and Christian Ethics.* New York: Cambridge University Press.

BIBLIOGRAPHY

———. 2000. *Family: A Christian Social Perspective.* Minneapolis: Fortress Press.

Cahill, Lisa Sowle, and Thomas A. Shannon. 1968. *Religion and Artificial Reproduction: An Inquiry into the Vatican "Instruction on Respect for Human Life.* New York: Crossroad.

Canon Law Society of America. 1983. *Code of Canon Law.* Washington, D.C.: Libreria Editrice Vaticana.

Childress, James F. 1986. "Order." In *The Westminster Dictionary of Christian Ethics,* ed. James F. Childress and John Macquarrie, 439–440. Philadelphia: Westminster Press.

———. 1997. "Moral Rhetoric and Moral Reasoning: Some Reflections on Evangelium Vitae." In *Choosing Life: A Dialogue on Evangelium Vitae,* ed. Kevin Wm. Wildes, S.J., and Alan C. Mitchell, 21–36. Washington, D.C.: Georgetown University Press.

Clark, Elizabeth, ed. 1996. *St. Augustine on Marriage and Sexuality.* Washington, D.C.: Catholic University Press.

Congregation for the Doctrine of Faith. 1975. *Declaration on Sexual Ethics.*
———. 1987. *Donum Vitae (The Gift of Life).*
———. 2000. *Dominus Iesus (On the Unicity and Salvific Universality of Jesus Christ and the Church).*
———. 2003. *Considerations Regarding Proposals to Give Legal Recognition to Unions Between Homosexual Persons.*
Coughlan, Michael. 1990. *The Vatican, the Law, and the Human Embryo.* Iowa City: University of Iowa Press.
Curran, Charles. 1999. *The Catholic Moral Tradition Today: A Synthesis.* Washington, D.C.: Georgetown University Press.
———. 1992. "Sexual Ethics in the Roman Catholic Tradition." In *Religion and Sexual Health: Ethical, Theological, and Clinical Perspectives,* ed. Ronald M. Green, 17–35. Boston: Kluwer Academic Publishers.
Curran, Charles, and Richard McCormick, S.J., eds. "Statement by Catholic Theologians, Washington, D.C., July 30, 1968." In *Dialogue about Catholic Sexual Teaching,* 135–137. New York: Paulist Press.
Delhaye, Karl. 1964. *Ecclesia Mater Chez les Pères des Trois Premiers Siècles.* Paris: Latour-Maubourg, Les Éditions du Cerf 29.
Dulles, Avery. 1974. *Models of the Church.* Garden City, N.Y.: Doubleday.
Finnis, John. 1994. "Beyond the Encyclical." In *Considering Veritatis Splendor,* ed. John Wilkins, 69–76. Cleveland: Pilgrim Press.
Fiorenza, Elisabeth Schüssler. 1992. *In Memory of Her: A Feminist Theological Reconstruction of Christian Origins.* New York: Crossroad.
Fiorenza, Francis Schüssler. 2001. "Marriage." In *Sexuality, Marriage and Family: Readings in the Catholic Tradition,* ed. Paulinus Ikechukwu Odozor, 313–339. Notre Dame: University of Notre Dame Press.
Ford, John C. 1942. "Marriage: Its Meaning and Purposes." *Theological Studies* 3: 333–374.
Ford, John C., and Germain Grisez. 1988. *The Teaching of "Humanae vitae": A Defense.* San Francisco: Ignatius Press.
Ford, John C., and Gerald Kelly. 1964. *Contemporary Moral Theology.* Volume II. *Marriage Questions.* Westminster: The Newman Press.
France, David. 2004. *Our Fathers: The Secret Life of the Catholic Church in an Age of Scandal.* New York: Broadway Books.
Grabowski, John S. 2003. *Sex and Virtue: An Introduction to Sexual Ethics.* Washington, D.C.: Catholic University Press.
Gramick, Jeanine, and Pat Furey, eds. 1988. *The Vatican and Homosexuality.* New York: Crossroad.
Gudorf, Christine E. 1989. "Encountering the Other: The Modern Papacy on Women." *Social Compass* 36: 295–310.
———. 1994. *Body, Sex, and Pleasure: Reconstructing Christian Sexual Ethics.* Cleveland: Pilgrim Press.
Hammington, Maurice. 1995. *Hail Mary? The Struggle for Ultimate Womanhood in Catholicism.* New York: Routledge.
Häring, Bernard. 1967. "Fostering the Nobility of Marriage and the Family."

In *Commentary on the Documents of Vatican II,* vol. V, ed. Herbert Vorgrimler, 225–245. New York: Herder and Herder.

————. 1993. "The Inseparability of the Unitive-Procreative Functions of the Marital Act." In *Dialogue about Catholic Sexual Teaching,* ed. Charles E. Curran and Richard A. McCormick, S.J., 153–167. New York: Paulist Press.

Hogan, Margaret Monahan. 1993. *Finality and Marriage.* Marquette: Marquette University Press.

Hoose, Bernard. 1987. *Proportionalism: The American Debate and Its European Roots.* Washington, D.C.: Georgetown University Press.

Horgan, John, ed. 1972. *Humanae Vitae and the Bishops: The Encyclical and the Statements of the National Hierarchies.* Shannon: Irish University Press.

Hughes, Gerard. 1986. "Totality, Principle of." In *Westminster Dictionary of Christian Ethics,* ed. James F. Childress and John Mcquarrie, 629. Philadelphia: Westminster Press.

International Theological Commission. 1999. *Memory and Reconciliation: The Church and the Faults of the Past.* Available online at http://www.vatican.va/roman_curia/congregations/cfaith/cti_documents/rc_con_cfaith_doc_20000307_memory-reconc-itc_en.html.

Isherwood, Lisa, ed. 2000. *The Good News of the Body: Sexual Theology and Feminism.* New York: New York University Press.

Jannsens, Louis. 1979. "Ontic Evil and Moral Evil." In *Moral Norms and Catholic Tradition,* ed. Charles Curran and Richard A. McCormick, 40–93. Mahwah: Paulist Press.

John Paul II, Pope. 1981. *Familiaris Consortio (The Role of the Christian Family in the Modern World).* Boston: St. Paul's Books and Media.

————. 1985. *Dolentium Hominum (Establishing Pontifical Commission for the Apostolate of Health Care Workers).* Available online at http://www.vatican.va/holy_father/john_paul_ii/moto_proprio/index.htm.

————. 1987. *Redemptoris Mater (Mother of the Redeemer).* Boston: St. Paul's Books and Media.

————. 1988. *Mulieres Dignitatem (On the Dignity and Vocation of Women).* Boston: St. Paul's Books and Media.

————. 1993. *Veritatis Splendor (The Splendor of Truth).* Boston: St. Paul's Books and Media.

————. 1994. *Tertio Millennio Adveniente.* Available online at http://www.vatican.va/holy_father/john_paul_ii/apost_letters/documents/hf_jp-ii_apl_10111994_tertio-millennio-adveniente_en.html.

————. 1995a. *Evangelium Vitae (The Gospel of Life).* New York: Random House.

————. 1995b. Letter to Women. Available online at http://www.vatican.va/holy_father/john_paul_ii/letters/documents/hf_jp-ii_let_29061995_women_en.html.

————. 1997. *The Theology of the Body: Human Love in the Divine Plan.* Boston: Pauline Books and Media.

————. 2003. "Address to the Members of the Pontifical Academy of Sciences, 10 November 2003." Available online at http://www.vatican.va/holy_father/john_paul_ii/speeches/2003/november/documents/hf_jp-ii_spe_20031110_academy-sciences_en.html.

Johnson, Elizabeth A., C.S.J. 1992. "The Marian Tradition and the Reality of Women." In *Horizons on Catholic Feminist Theology*, ed. Joann Wolski Conn and Walter E. Conn, 85–107. Washington, D.C.: Georgetown University Press.

Jordan, Mark D. 2000. *The Silence of Sodom: Homosexuality and Modern Catholicism*. Chicago: University of Chicago Press.

————. 2002. *The Ethics of Sex*. Oxford: Blackwell Publishers.

Jung, Patricia Beattie, ed. 2001. *Sexual Diversity and Catholicism: Toward the Development of Moral Theology*. Collegeville: Liturgical Press.

Kaczor, Christopher. 1999. "Proportionalism and the Pill: How Developments in Theory Lead to Contradictions in Practice." *The Thomist* 63: 269–281.

Kaiser, Robert Blair. 1985. *The Politics of Sex and Religion: A Case History in the Development of Doctrine, 1962–1984*. Kansas City: Leaven Press.

Kalbian, Aline H. 2001. "The Catholic Church's Public Confession: Theological and Ethical Implications." *Annual of the Society of Christian Ethics* 21: 175–189.

————. 2002. "Where Have All the Proportionalists Gone?" *Journal of Religious Ethics* 30, no. 1: 1–22.

Laqueur, Thomas. 1990. *Making Sex: Body and Gender from the Greeks to Freud*. Cambridge, Mass.: Harvard University Press.

Lauritzen, Paul. 2003. "A Consistent Rhetoric of Life?" Unpublished manuscript.

Liebard, Odile M. 1978. *Official Catholic Teachings: Love and Sexuality*. Wilmington, N.C.: McGrath Publishing Company (A Consortium Book).

Little, David. 1969. *Religion, Order, and Law: A Study in Pre-Revolutionary England*. New York: Harper and Row.

McAlister, Elizabeth. 2000. "Love, Sex, and Gender Embodied: The Spirits of Haitian Vodou." In *Love, Sex, and Gender in the World's Religions*, ed. Joseph Runzo and Nancy M. Martin. Oxford: Oneworld Publications.

McBrien, Richard P. 1994. *Catholicism*. Rev. ed. San Francisco: Harper.

McCormick, Richard A., S.J. 1989a. "Moral Theology 1940–1989: An Overview." *Theological Studies* 50: 3–24.

————. 1989b. *The Critical Calling: Reflections on Moral Dilemmas since Vatican II*. Washington, D.C.: Georgetown University Press, 1989.

————. 1990. "The First Fourteen Days." *The Tablet*, March 10.

McClory, Robert. 1995. *Turning Point: The Inside Story of the Papal Birth Control Commission and How* Humanae Vitae *Changed the Life of Patty Crowley and the Future of the Church*. New York: Crossroad.

Mackin, Theodore. 1982. *What Is Marriage?* New York: Paulist Press.

————. 1989. *The Marital Sacrament*. New York: Paulist Press.

Mahoney, John. 1987. *The Making of Moral Theology: A Study of the Roman Catholic Tradition*. Oxford: Clarendon, Oxford University Press.

Melady, Margaret B. 1999. *The Rhetoric of John Paul II: The Pastoral Visit as a New Vocabulary of the Sacred*. Westport: Praeger.

Miller, Richard. 1996. *Casuistry and Modern Ethics: A Poetics of Practical Reasoning*. Chicago: University of Chicago Press.

Moore, Gareth. 1992. *The Body in Context: Sex and Catholicism*. London: SCM Press.

Newman, John Henry. 1989. *An Essay on the Development of Christian Doctrine*. 6th ed. Notre Dame, Ind.: University of Notre Dame Press.

Noonan, John. 1966. *Contraception: A History of Its Treatment by the Catholic Theologians and Canonists*. Cambridge, Mass.: Harvard University Press.

————. 1993. "A Development in Doctrine." *Theological Studies* 54: 662–677.

Novak, Michael, ed. 1964. *The Experience of Marriage: The Testimony of Catholic Laymen*. New York: Macmillan Company.

O'Brien, David J , and Thomas A. Shannon, eds. 1992. *Catholic Social Teaching: A Documentary Heritage*. New York: Orbis.

Patrick, Ann. 1993. "Veritatis Splendor." *Commonweal*. 120: 18.

Paul VI, Pope. 1968. *Humanae Vitae (Of Human Life)*. Boston: St. Paul's Books and Media.

Pius XI, Pope. 1930. *Casti Connubii (On Christian Marriage)*. Boston: St. Paul's Books and Media.

Plaskow, Judith. 2000. "Decentering Sex: Rethinking Jewish Sexual Ethics." In *God Forbid: Religion and Sex in American Public Life,* ed. Kathleen Sands, 23–41. New York: Oxford University Press.

Plumpe, Joseph C. 1943. *Mater Ecclesia: An Inquiry into the Concept of Church as Mother in Early Christianity*. Washington, D.C.: Catholic University Press.

Pontifical Council for the Family. 1995. *The Truth and Meaning of Human Sexuality: Guidelines for Education with the Family*. Available online at http://www.vatican.va/roman_curia/pontifical_councils/family/documents/rc_pc_family_doc_08121995_human-sexuality_en.html.

Quay, Paul M., S.J. 1985. *The Christian Meaning of Human Sexuality*. San Francisco: Ignatius Press.

Rogers, Eugene. 1999. *Sexuality and the Christian Body*. Oxford: Blackwell.

Ross, Susan A. 1991. "The Bride of Christ and the Body Politic: Body and Gender in Pre-Vatican II Marriage Theology." *The Journal of Religion* 71, no. 3: 345–361.

————. 1992. " 'Then Honor God in Your Body' (1 Cor. 6:20): Feminist and Sacramental Theology on the Body." In *Horizons on Catholic Feminist Theology,* ed. Joann Wolski Conn and Walter E. Conn, 109–132. Washington, D.C.: Georgetown University Press.

————. 1998. *Extravagant Affections: A Feminist Sacramental Theology*. New York: Continuum.

―――――. 2001. "The Bridegroom and the Bride: The Theological Anthropology of John Paul II and Its Relation to the Bible and Homosexuality." In *Sexual Diversity and Catholicism,* ed. Patricia Beattie Jung, 39–59. Collegeville, Minn.: Liturgical Press.

Ruether, Rosemary Radford. 1983. *Sexism and God Talk: Toward a Feminist Theology.* Boston: Beacon Press.

―――――. 1991. "Feminist Hermeneutics, Scriptural Authority, and Religious Experience: The Case of the *Imago Dei* and Gender Equality." In *Radical Pluralism and Truth: David Tracy and the Hermeneutics of Religion,* ed. Werner G. Jeanrond and Jennifer L. Rike, 95–106. New York: Crossroad.

Ryan, John A. 1920. *A Living Wage: Its Ethical and Economic Aspects.* New York: Macmillan.

Ryan, Maura A. 2001. *The Ethics and Economics of Assisted Reproduction: The Cost of Longing.* Washington, D.C.: Georgetown University Press.

Sands, Kathleen. 2000. "Public, Pubic, and Private: Religion in Political Discourse." In *God Forbid: Religion and Sex in American Public Life,* ed. Kathleen Sands. New York: Oxford University Press.

Secker, Susan L. 1993. "Human Experience and Women's Experience: Resources for Catholic Ethics." In *Dialogue about Catholic Sexual Teaching,* ed. Charles E. Curran and Richard A. McCormick, 577–599. New York: Paulist Press.

Selling, Joseph A. 1998. "The 'Meanings' of Human Sexuality." *Louvain Studies* 23: 22–37.

Sullivan, Francis, A. 1983. *Magisterium: Teaching Authority in the Catholic Church.* New York: Paulist Press.

―――――. 2000. "The Papal Apology." *America* 18, no. 12: 17–22.

Traina, Cristina L. H. 1997. "Oh, Susanna: The New Absolutism and Natural Law." *Journal of the American Academy of Religion* 65, no. 2: 371–401.

―――――. 1999. *Feminist Ethics and Natural Law: The End of the Anathemas.* Washington, D.C.: Georgetown University Press.

United States Catholic Conference. 1994. *Catechism of the Catholic Church for the United States of America.* Mahwah: Paulist Press.

Weaver, Mary Jo. 1995. *New Catholic Women: A Contemporary Challenge to Traditional Religious Authority.* Bloomington: Indiana University Press.

Weber, Leonhard. 1967. "Excursus on Humanae Vitae." In *Commentary on the Documents of Vatican II,* vol. V, ed. Herbert Vorgrimler, 397–402. New York: Herder and Herder.

Wills, Garry. 2000. *Structures of Deceit: Papal Sin.* New York: Doubleday.

Wojtyla, Karol (Pope John Paul II). 1981. *Love and Responsibility.* Rev. ed. Translated by H. T. Willetts. New York: Farrar, Strauss, Giroux.

abortion: church teachings about, 33, 40, 121–123, 150nn16,18; debate about, within Catholic Church, 2, 34

Adam and Eve, 3, 24, 25, 27, 128

"Address to the Midwives," 57, 61

adultery, 45–46, 48

Aelred of Rivaulx, 110

Anglican Church: lifts ban on contraceptives in 1930, 33–34; ratification of use of oral contraceptives in 1958, 57

Anselm of Canterbury, 109–110

Apostolicam Actuositatem (1965), 146n14

Arcanum Diviniae Sapientiae (1880): on gender roles within marriage, 56, 98; on marriage as a sacrament, 25; mentioned, 6, 22, 33, 46. *See also* Leo XIII

artificial insemination, 70, 76. *See also* assisted reproductive technologies; cloning; in vitro fertilization; stem-cell research; surrogate motherhood

Augustine, Saint: on chastity, 47; influence on church teachings about marriage, 33, 53, 77, 107, 146n12; and marriage as sacrament, 23–24; on order, 2–3, 92, 143n6; rejection of sexual pleasure by, 34, 147n18; on sterile couples, 38

Balthasar, Hans Urs von, 107, 153n10

Bernard of Clairvaux, 109

bioethics, Catholic, 66

birth control, 77–78. *See also* coitus interruptus; condoms; contraception; diaphragms; eugenics; oral contraceptives; pill; rhythm method; sterilization

Bouyer, Louis, 107

Butler, Judith, 14, 105

Bynum, Caroline Walker, 12–13, 109–110, 132

Cahill, Lisa, 15–17, 83, 129–130

Casti Connubii (1930): on adultery, 45–47; on blessings of marriage,

assisted reproduction, 16, 78, 80, 81, 82, 85, 121; and inseparability of ends, 88; questions raised by, 94

assisted reproductive technologies, 2, 17, 39, 70–71, 150n16; and concern for embryos, 74, and human dominion over nature, 75; and sanctity of procreative sex, 74–75; and views of Congregation for the Doctrine of Faith and, 72–77; and views of Pius XII, 69–72. *See also* artificial insemination; cloning; in vitro fertilization; stem-cell research; surrogate motherhood

Association for Large Families of Italy, 39

Association for Large Families of Rome, 39

31; challenged by *Gaudium et Spes,* 58; on chastity within marriage, 43–45; compared with *Donum Vitae,* 73; compared with *Humanae Vitae,* 68; on contraception as a sin against nature, 62–63, on divorce, 26; as major Catholic document on marriage and procreation, 35; on marriage as a sacrament, 28–29; and metaphor of adopting mother, 118; on motherhood, 36; and principle of totality, 91; on procreation as end of marriage, 33, 56–57; and self-control, 140–141; on sexual pleasure within marriage, 44, 47; on sterilization, 91. *See also* Pius XI

celibacy, 50, 142, 146n16, 147n21

chastity: effects of, 50–51; within marriage, 17, 22, 43–45, 49, 128; synonyms for, 146n16
children: as a blessing of marriage, 33; as gifts from God, 35–36
Clark, Elizabeth, 33
cloning, 150n16. *See also* artificial insemination; assisted reproductive technologies; in vitro fertilization; stem-cell research; surrogate motherhood
Code of Canon Law, 81
coitus interruptus, 61. *See also* birth control; condoms; contraception; diaphragms; eugenics; oral contraceptives; pill; rhythm method; sterilization
condoms, 79. *See also* birth control; coitus interruptus; contraception; diaphragms; eugenics; oral contraceptives; pill; rhythm method; sterilization
Congregation for the Doctrine of Faith, 50; and assisted reproductive technologies, 72
Considerations Regarding Proposals to Give Legal Recognition to Unions Between Homosexual Persons (2003), 137–138
contraception: arguments against, 66, 84–85, 90, 95; and *Casti Connubii*, 33, 56; Catholic debate about, 2, 41, 55, 58, 83; Catholic teachings and, 23, 34, 37, 39, 58–59, 78, 80–82; and *Humanae Vitae,* 10, 95; and intrinsically evil acts, 82–83; natural versus artificial, 67; non-Catholic Christian churches and, 29, 34 (*see also* Anglican Church); questions raised by, 94; and views of Papal Birth Control Commission, 62–64. *See also* birth control; coitus interruptus; condoms; eugenics; oral contraceptives; pill; rhythm method; Second Vatican Council; sterilization
Crowley, Patty, 61, 64. *See also* Papal Birth Control Commission

cultural construction: of gender, 12, 14, 19; of sex, 14, 19
Curran, Charles, 7–8

death penalty, 121
Declaration on Certain Questions Concerning Sexual Ethics (1975), 50
Decree on the Apostolate of the Laity. See Apostolicam Actuositatem
Delhaye, Philippe, 61
diaphragms, 79. *See also* birth control; coitus interruptus; condoms; contraception; eugenics; oral contraceptives; pill; rhythm method; sterilization
divorce, 28, 48, 145n7
Dogmatic Constitution of the Church, 110. *See also Lumen Gentium*
Doms, Herbert, 42
Donum Vitae (1987): on assisted reproduction, 72, 75–76; and concern for embryos, 72, 74; on dignity of human person, 60, 68; and inseparability of ends, 84–85; mentioned, 151n25; and natural law, 73, 75, 79, 89, 92; and principle of totality, 91. *See also* assisted reproductive technologies
Dulles, Avery, 111

embryos, 150nn18–19; Catholic teachings and, 72, 74
Enlightenment, and changing definitions of male-female relations, 105
Eucharist, 113
eugenics, 33, 34, 91; contraception and, 38
euthanasia, 121
Evangelium Vitae (1995): and contraception, 68; on motherhood and spirituality, 103, 120–123; prohibits assisted reproductive technologies, 72

Familiaris Consortio, 68, 88, 120
family wage, 48, 147n20
Federation of Italian Women, 99

Fiorenza, Francis Schüssler, 114
Ford, John C., 41–42, 58, 146n12
France, David, 142

Gaudium et Spes (1965): and centrality of family for human well-being, 39; challenges Casti Connubii, 58; and contraception, 59; and responsible parenthood, 61; and sexuality within marriage, 41
gender: Catholic theology and, 2, 5, 9; cultural construction of, 12, 14, 19; definitions of, 13–17, 105–106, 143n8; and equality within marriage, 96; feminist analysis of, 12, 14; identity, 27, 53; and order, 5, 19, 20; as a stable biological category, 97. See also Enlightenment
gender complementarity, 9, 12, 18, 105–108, 127, 133, 152nn6–8; and inequality, 106–107; similarity to principle of inseparability of ends, 96–97; within marriage, 98–100, 102
Grabowski, John, 137
Great Jubilee of the Year 2000, 124, 126
Gudorf, Christine: critique of Augustinian view of sexuality, 147n18; critique of Pope John Paul II's teachings on women, 107, 152–153n9

Häring, Bernard, 38, 60–61, 148n6
hierarchy: and Catholic Church, 8; and family life, 3; gender and, 11, 15–16; within marriage, 96, 97–98, 114
Hildebrand, Dietrich von, 42
Holocaust, 124–125, 155n27. See also Memory and Reconciliation
homosexuality, 2, 137–141; and adoption of children, 150–151n23. See also Considerations Regarding Proposals to Give Legal Recognition to Unions Between Homosexual Persons; same-sex marriage

Humanae Vitae (1968): on contraception, 10, 65–67; critiques of, 108–109, 151n30; on dignity of the human person, 60; on inseparability of ends, 84–86; on marriage as expression of order, 22; mentioned, 35, 64; and natural law, 73, 80, 89, 92; on order, 79; and principle of totality, 90–91; rejects recommendations of Papal Birth Control Commission, 64; on rhythm method, 68; seen as betrayal of Vatican II, 69; on sexual pleasure within marriage, 95–96; as source of debate within Catholic Church, 65, 68–69, 77

impotence, 81–82, 151n35. See also "sterile" couples
in vitro fertilization, 70–71, 75–76, 151n35. See also artificial insemination; assisted reproductive technologies; cloning; stem-cell research; surrogate motherhood
inseparability of ends, 84–86, and assisted reproductive technology, 87, and contraception, 87, Familiaris Consortio and, 88; and gender complementarity, 96; and order, 89
International Convention of Catholic Physicians, 70
International Theological Commission, 124–125
Italian Catholic Association of Midwives, 35

Jahwist account of Bible, 101, 153n10
John XXIII, Pope, 56, 58, 119, 121
John Paul II, Pope: on assisted reproduction, 72; on celibacy, 50; on Church as bride of Christ, 114, 128; on Church as mother, 124–125, 127; on contraception, 68; on equality of women, 4–5; on gender complementarity, 19, 100–105, 108, 129; on gender equity

John Paul II, Pope (*continued*)
within marriage, 96; on inseparability of ends, 86–87; on marriage
as a sacrament, 26–27, 31; on
motherhood, 107–108, 115, 120;
on natural law, 91–92; on procreation, 75; on sacraments, 24; on
sexual pleasure within marriage,
48–49, 54, 145n8. *See also Considerations Regarding Proposals to Give
Legal Recognition to Unions Between
Homosexual Persons; Evangelium
Vitae; Love and Responsibility;
Memory and Reconciliation; Mulieres
Dignitatem; Redemptoris Mater; Tertio Millennio Adveniente; Veritatis
Splendor*
Jordan, Mark, 1, 15–17, 134–135,
143n8, 155n1

Kaiser, Robert, 57
Kant, Immanuel, 27
Kelly, Gerald, 41–42, 58, 146n12
Krempel, Bernhardin, 42

Lambeth conference (1930), 33. *See
also* Anglican Church
Lambruschini, Monsignor Ferdinando, 64–65
Laqueur, Thomas, 105–106
lay apostolate, 146n14
Leo XIII, Pope: on abuse of power
within marriage, 27–28; on
Church as bride of Christ, 26; on
church-state relations regarding
marriage, 56; on family and just
social order, 39; on gender complementarity, 98; on marriage as a
sacrament, 25; mentioned, 6, 22–
23, 29, 33, 35, 62; on procreation
within marriage, 145n5; on
threats to marriage, 48. *See also
Arcanum Diviniae Sapientiae; Rerum Novarum*
Letter to Women (1995), 100–102
Little, David, 4
Love and Responsibility, 48–49, 145n8
Lumen Gentium (1964), 110–113,

117–118, 124–125. *See also* Dogmatic Constitution on the Church

Mahoney, John, 7, 92
marriage: blessings within, 31, 33;
Catholic theology and, 4, 6, 8,
21; chastity within, 17, 22, 43–45,
49; companionship as the end of,
41; equality within, 96; and es-
chatology, 30–31; gender complementarity within, 98–100, 102;
and order, 11, 21–22; as process,
26; Protestant views of, 40–42; as
sacrament, 17, 20–31, 47, 52,
128, 131–132, 144n2; sexual
pleasure within, 47–49, 95–96;
women's oppression within, 27–
28. *See also* papal encyclicals; procreation
Mater et Magistra (1961), 119, 121
McAlister, Elizabeth, 19
McBrien, Richard, 83
McClory, Robert, 61, 149nn8,10.
See also Papal Birth Control Commission
Melady, Margaret, 108
*Memory and Reconciliation: The Church
and the Faults of the Past* (1994),
124
metaphors for Catholic Church: as
adopting mother, 118–119; as
body of Christ, 111–113; as bride
of Christ, 19, 22, 95, 113–115,
128, 131; as a building, 110–111;
as a family, 129–130; as female,
18–19; as Mary, 115–118; as
mother, 12, 95, 110–112, 116,
119–127, 130; as the people of
God, 112; as a sheepfold, 110–
111; as teacher, 119, 121–122; as
a vineyard, 110–111; as a virgin,
95, 117, 125–126. *See also* sexing
the Church as female
midwives, 35–37
Miller, Richard, 108–110
Moore, Gareth, 32
Mulieres Dignitatem (1988), 102–103,
114, 128

natural law: *Donum Vitae* and, 73–74; and prohibition of contraception, 62–63

Noonan, John, 23, 38, 81–82, 144n3. *See also* Papal Birth Control Commission

oral contraceptives, 57–58, 148n4. *See also* birth control; coitus interruptus; condoms; contraception; diaphragms; eugenics; pill; rhythm method; sterilization

order, 2–3, 19–20; Catholic theology and, 6–8; and Catholic views of homosexuality, 139–140; and church authority, 21; and gender, 11, 21; and marriage, 11, 21–22; and reproduction, 77–78; and sexuality, 12, 21, 51; and sexual-abuse scandal within Church, 140–142

Papal Birth Control Commission: concern of, about intrinsic evil of contraception, 61, 83; described, 149n8; mentioned, 55; models for, 147–148n2; pope rejects recommendations of, 60; report of, 149nn7,10 (*see also Schema for a Document on Responsible Parenthood*). *See also* Crowley, Patty; McClory, Robert; Noonan, John; *Turning Point*

papal encyclicals. *See Apostolicam Actuositatem; Arcanum Diviniae Sapientiae; Casti Connubii; Evangelium Vitae; Humanae Vitae; Mater et Magistra; Redemptoris Mater; Veritatis Splendor*

Pastoral Constitution on the Church in the Modern World. See Gaudium et Spes

patriarchy, and *Humanae Vitae,* 108–109

Paul VI, Pope: on contraception, 10, 64–68, 90; on marriage as expression of order, 22; on procreation, 88; rejects recommendations of

Papal Birth Control Commission, 60; on sexual pleasure within marriage, 95–96. *See also Humanae Vitae*

Persona Humana. See Declaration on Certain Questions Concerning Sexual Ethics

personalism: and challenge to hierarchy within marriage, 152n6; in *Donum Vitae,* 60; in *Gaudium et Spes,* 60; in *Humanae Vitae,* 60, 84; influence on Catholic views of sexuality, 51; and natural law, 106–107; Pope John Paul II on, 49; in report of the Papal Birth Control Commission, 63; and Second Vatican Council, 42

pill, 67, 79, 148n4. *See also* birth control; coitus interruptus; condoms; contraception; diaphragms; eugenics; oral contraceptives; rhythm method; sterilization

Pius II, Pope, 40

Pius XI, Pope: on chastity within marriage, 34, 44–47, 62, 140–141; on children within marriage, 36–37; on church-state relations regarding marriage, 29; on Church as mother, 118; on contraception, 37, 56–58, 60, 68; on divorce, 26; on marriage as a sacrament, 28–29; on order, 6, 21; on principal of totality, 90–91; on procreation as the end of marriage, 33; on role of midwives, 35–37; on sterilization, 34–35, 91; on threats to marriage, 48; on women's subordination to men, 4, 46, 98. *See also Casti Connubii*

Pius XII, Pope: on contraception, 37–38, 57, 60, 62; on different purposes of children for men and women, 32, 36–37; and gender complementarity, 99–100; on procreation as the end of marriage, 35, 58; theory of family life, 39–40; views on celibacy, 147n21; on widowhood, 30, 113

Plumpe, Joseph, 125–126
Pontifical Council for the Family, 51, 106
post–Vatican II period, 2, 4, 34
pre–Vatican II period, 4, 23, 98
Priestly account of Bible, 101, 153n10
procreation, as end of marriage, 17, 21–22, 31–43, 49, 52–53, 58–59, 74. *See also* "sterile" couples

Quay, Paul, 131–132

Ratzinger, Cardinal Joseph, 72
Redemptoris Mater (1987), 115–117
Rerum Novarum (1891), 39, 145n5
responsible parenthood, 59–60, 66. *See also Schema for a Document on Responsible Parenthood*
rhythm method, 61, 67–68. *See also* birth control; coitus interruptus; condoms; contraception; diaphragms; eugenics; oral contraceptives; pill; sterilization
Rogers, Eugene, 32, 146n11
Ross, Susan, 19, 24–25, 43, 98, 106–107
Ruether, Rosemary Radford, 5, 143n5
Ryan, Maura, 85

Saigh, Patriarch Maximos IV, 55, 148n3
same-sex marriage, 137–141, 146n11. *See also Considerations Regarding Proposals to Give Legal Recognition to Unions Between Homosexual Persons;* homosexuality
sanctity of life, 40
Sands, Kathleen, 143n1
Schema for a Document on Responible Parenthood, 60–64. *See also* Papal Birth Control Commission
Second Vatican Council: and crisis of authority in Catholic Church, 18; and contraception, 58; examines sexuality within marriage, 41, 55, 58–60; and introduction of meta-phor of Church as people of God, 112; and lay apostolate, 146n11; personalism of documents of, 63; theologians' use of, to criticize *Humanae Vitae,* 69. *See also Gaudium et Spes; Lumen Gentium;* Papal Birth Control Commission; post–Vatican II period; pre–Vatican II period; *Schema for a Document on Responsible Parenthood;* Vatican II
Second World Congress on Fertility and Sterility, 70
self-mastery, 52, 86
Selling, Joseph, 95; critique of *Humanae Vitae,* 151n30
Seventh International Hematological Congress, 57, 148n4
sex, definitions of, 13–17, 143n8; feminist analysis of, 14
sexing the Church as female: and Catholic attitudes about gender, 95, 114; and challenge to order, 5, 7, 9–11, 18, 129–131; consequences of for priesthood, 142; consequences of for sexual-abuse scandal within Church, 142; John Paul II's views on, 128–129; and women's inequality, 131–132. *See also* metaphors for Catholic Church
sexual pleasure: celibacy and, 147n21; St. Augustine's views on, 147n18; and tension with procreation in Church teachings, 18, 34, 37–38; within marriage, 47–49, 95–96
sexual-abuse scandal within Church, 139–141
Shrine of Loretto, 99
stem-cell research, 150n16. *See also* artificial insemination; assisted reproductive technologies; cloning; in vitro fertilization; surrogate motherhood
"sterile" couples, 11, 38, 67, 71, 81–82
sterilization, 33, 35, 48, 91, 148n4. *See also* birth control; coitus inter-

ruptus; condoms; contraception; diaphragms; eugenics; oral contraceptives; pill; rhythm method

Suenens, Cardinal Leo Joseph, 55, 147–148n2

Sullivan, Francis, 126

surrogate motherhood, 76. *See also* artificial insemination; assisted reproductive technologies; cloning; in vitro fertilization; stem-cell research

Tertio Millennio Adveniente (1994), 124, 126

Thomas Aquinas, Saint, 15, 31, 92, 107

totality, principle of: and arguments against contraception, 90; and *Casti Connubii,* 91; development of, 151n35; and *Donum Vitae,* 91; and *Humanae Vitae,* 91; and physical body, 89–91; and society, 89; and *Veritatis Splendor,* 92

Turning Point, 61

utilitarianism, 1

Vatican II: and gender equity within marriage, 96; *Humanae Vitae* seen as a betrayal of, 69; and introduction of Church as people of God, 8; spirit of democracy at, 60. *See also* post–Vatican II period; pre–Vatican II period; Second Vatican Council

Veritatis Splendor (1993), 1–2, 68,

120–124, 127; and principle of totality, 92

Virgin Mary: centrality of, in lives of priests, 127; and complementarity, 99; as illustration of sexuality/chastity dualism, 12, 104; as model for a moral life, 121; and motherhood, 113, 115–117, 122; sanctity of, 125

virginity: and metaphor for Catholic Church, 11–12; and women as property, 154n23

Voice of the Faithful, 139

Weaver, Mary Jo, 107

William of St. Thierry, 110

Wills, Gary, 127

Wojtyla, Karol, 48–49. *See also* John Paul II

women's oppression: associated with paganism, 99–100; and Catholic Church, 109; within marriage, 27–28

women's ordination, 2, 104

women's rights, and Catholic Church, 18, 46–47, 100

women's roles, as caretakers, 12; as helpers to men, 99; as mothers, 12, 100–105; as receptive vessels, 104; as sufferers, 113, 123; as widows, 30–31

World Union of Family Organizations, 30

Yahwist account of Bible, 101, 153n10

Zalba, Marcelino, 61

ALINE H. KALBIAN is Assistant Professor of Religion at Florida State University.